OPPOSING
VIEWPOINTS®
SERIES

Religious Liberty

Other Books of Related Interest:

Opposing Viewpoints Series

American Values

Civil Liberties

At Issue Series

Polygamy

Current Controversies Series

Politics and Religion

"Congress shall make
no law ... abridging
the freedom of speech,
or of the press."

First Amendment to the US Constitution

The basic foundation of our democracy is the First Amendment guarantee of freedom of expression. The Opposing Viewpoints Series is dedicated to the concept of this basic freedom and the idea that it is more important to practice it than to enshrine it.

Religious Liberty

Carol Ullmann and Lynn M. Zott, Book Editors

GREENHAVEN PRESS
A part of Gale, Cengage Learning

Farmington Hills, Mich • San Francisco • New York • Waterville, Maine
Meriden, Conn • Mason, Ohio • Chicago

GALE
CENGAGE Learning

Elizabeth Des Chenes, *Director, Content Strategy*
Douglas Dentino, *Manager, New Product*

© 2014 Greenhaven Press, a part of Gale, Cengage Learning.

WCN: 01-100-101

Gale and Greenhaven Press are registered trademarks used herein under license.

For more information, contact:
Greenhaven Press
27500 Drake Rd.
Farmington Hills, MI 48331-3535
Or you can visit our Internet site at gale.cengage.com

For product information and technology assistance, contact us at

Gale Customer Support, 1-800-877-4253
For permission to use material from this text or product, submit all requests online at
www.cengage.com/permissions

Further permissions questions can be emailed to permissionrequest@cengage.com

Articles in Greenhaven Press anthologies are often edited for length to meet page requirements. In addition, original titles of these works are changed to clearly present the main thesis and to explicitly indicate the author's opinion. Every effort is made to ensure that Greenhaven Press accurately reflects the original intent of the authors. Every effort has been made to trace the owners of copyrighted material.

Cover image copyright © Maria Dryfhout/Shutterstock.com.

LIBRARY OF CONGRESS CATALOGING-IN-PUBLICATION DATA

Religious liberty (Greenhaven Press)
  Religious liberty / Carol Ullmann and Lynn M. Zott, Book Editor.
      pages cm. -- (Opposing viewpoints)
  Summary: "Opposing Viewpoints: Religious Liberty: Opposing Viewpoints is the leading source for libraries and classrooms in need of current-issue materials. The viewpoints are selected from a wide range of highly respected sources and publications"-- Provided by publisher.
  Includes bibliographical references and index.
  ISBN 978-0-7377-6664-6 (hardback) -- ISBN 978-0-7377-6665-3 (paperback)
  1. Freedom of religion--United States--Juvenile literature. 2. Religion and state--United States--Juvenile literature. I. Ullmann, Carol, editor of compilation. II. Zott, Lynn M. (Lynn Marie), 1969- editor of compilation. III. Title.
  BR516.R43 2014
  323.44'20973--dc23
                                                                    2014003361

Printed in the United States of America
1 2 3 4 5 6 7 18 17 16 15 14

Contents

Why Consider Opposing Viewpoints?   11

Introduction   14

Chapter 1: Why Is Religious Liberty Important and Controversial?

Chapter Preface   18

1. Religious Liberty Is Essential to Ensure   20
   a Free Society
   Jennifer A. Marshall

2. The "Religious Liberty" Bullies and Their   28
   Fight Against LGBT Equality
   Jay Michaelson

3. In Defense of Religious Liberty   34
   Ken Blackwell

4. The United States Was Founded   38
   on Religious Liberty
   Charles J. Chaput

5. Religious Liberty Promotes World   44
   Peace and Equity
   Silvano M. Tomasi

Periodical and Internet Sources Bibliography   54

Chapter 2: What Does the US Constitution Say About Religious Liberty?

Chapter Preface   56

1. The US Constitution Provides Clear   58
   Protections for Religious Liberty
   Melissa Moschella

2. The US Constitution Does Not Guarantee   65
   Religious Liberty
   Monte Kuligowski

3. The US Constitution Guarantees Freedom   71
   from Religion
   Tony Houston

4. Interpreting the First Amendment's Commentary   77
   on Religious Liberty Is Inherently Complex
   John Coleman

5. Restricting Religious Expression in Schools   86
   Is Constitutional
   Anti-Defamation League

6. Restricting Religious Expression in Schools   94
   Is Unconstitutional
   Alliance Defending Freedom

Periodical and Internet Sources Bibliography   102

Chapter 3: Is Religious Liberty Under Threat?

Chapter Preface   104

1. Legally Mandated Birth Control Coverage   106
   Violates Employers' Religious Liberty
   Alan Sears

2. Legally Mandated Birth Control Coverage Does   111
   Not Violate Employers' Religious Liberty
   Barry W. Lynn

3. American Muslims' Religious Liberty   116
   Is Threatened by Surveillance
   Conor Friedersdorf

4. Legalizing Abortion Endangers Religious Liberty   127
   Mark Pattison

Periodical and Internet Sources Bibliography   132

Chapter 4: What Is the Impact of Politics on Religious Liberty?

Chapter Preface   134

1. Liberal and Progressive Politics Protect   135
   Religious Liberty and Democracy
   Marta Cook and John Halpin

2. Religious Liberty Damages Religion   141
   Benjamin Wiker

3. Conservative Politics Protect Religious Liberty   152
   David Limbaugh

4. Conservatives' Use of Religious Liberty as a   157
   Political Issue Threatens Democracy
   Jay Michaelson

5. Religion and Politics Must Remain Separate   166
   to Preserve Religious Liberty
   Sara Hutchinson

6. Separation of Religion and Politics Endangers   173
   Religious Liberty
   David Green

Periodical and Internet Sources Bibliography   177
For Further Discussion   178
Organizations to Contact   180
Bibliography of Books   184
Index   187

Why Consider Opposing Viewpoints?

> "The only way in which a human being can make some approach to knowing the whole of a subject is by hearing what can be said about it by persons of every variety of opinion and studying all modes in which it can be looked at by every character of mind. No wise man ever acquired his wisdom in any mode but this."
>
> *John Stuart Mill*

In our media-intensive culture it is not difficult to find differing opinions. Thousands of newspapers and magazines and dozens of radio and television talk shows resound with differing points of view. The difficulty lies in deciding which opinion to agree with and which "experts" seem the most credible. The more inundated we become with differing opinions and claims, the more essential it is to hone critical reading and thinking skills to evaluate these ideas. Opposing Viewpoints books address this problem directly by presenting stimulating debates that can be used to enhance and teach these skills. The varied opinions contained in each book examine many different aspects of a single issue. While examining these conveniently edited opposing views, readers can develop critical thinking skills such as the ability to compare and contrast authors' credibility, facts, argumentation styles, use of persuasive techniques, and other stylistic tools. In short, the Opposing Viewpoints Series is an ideal way to attain the higher-level thinking and reading skills so essential in a culture of diverse and contradictory opinions.

In addition to providing a tool for critical thinking, Opposing Viewpoints books challenge readers to question their own strongly held opinions and assumptions. Most people form their opinions on the basis of upbringing, peer pressure, and personal, cultural, or professional bias. By reading carefully balanced opposing views, readers must directly confront new ideas as well as the opinions of those with whom they disagree. This is not to argue simplistically that everyone who reads opposing views will—or should—change his or her opinion. Instead, the series enhances readers' understanding of their own views by encouraging confrontation with opposing ideas. Careful examination of others' views can lead to the readers' understanding of the logical inconsistencies in their own opinions, perspective on why they hold an opinion, and the consideration of the possibility that their opinion requires further evaluation.

Evaluating Other Opinions

To ensure that this type of examination occurs, Opposing Viewpoints books present all types of opinions. Prominent spokespeople on different sides of each issue as well as well-known professionals from many disciplines challenge the reader. An additional goal of the series is to provide a forum for other, less known, or even unpopular viewpoints. The opinion of an ordinary person who has had to make the decision to cut off life support from a terminally ill relative, for example, may be just as valuable and provide just as much insight as a medical ethicist's professional opinion. The editors have two additional purposes in including these less known views. One, the editors encourage readers to respect others' opinions—even when not enhanced by professional credibility. It is only by reading or listening to and objectively evaluating others' ideas that one can determine whether they are worthy of consideration. Two, the inclusion of such viewpoints encourages the important critical thinking skill of objectively evaluating an author's credentials and bias. This evaluation will illuminate an author's reasons for taking a particular stance on an issue and will aid in readers' evaluation of the author's ideas.

It is our hope that these books will give readers a deeper understanding of the issues debated and an appreciation of the complexity of even seemingly simple issues when good and honest people disagree. This awareness is particularly important in a democratic society such as ours in which people enter into public debate to determine the common good. Those with whom one disagrees should not be regarded as enemies but rather as people whose views deserve careful examination and may shed light on one's own.

Thomas Jefferson once said that "difference of opinion leads to inquiry, and inquiry to truth." Jefferson, a broadly educated man, argued that "if a nation expects to be ignorant and free . . . it expects what never was and never will be." As individuals and as a nation, it is imperative that we consider the opinions of others and examine them with skill and discernment. The Opposing Viewpoints Series is intended to help readers achieve this goal.

David L. Bender and Bruno Leone,
Founders

Introduction

> "The Religion then of every man must be left to the conviction and conscience of every man; and it is the right of every man to exercise it as these may dictate. This right is in its nature an unalienable right."
>
> —James Madison,
> fourth president of the United States,
> 1809–1817

Religious liberty is one of the founding principles of the United States. Among the earliest colonists to arrive in the area of the New World that would later become the United States were Puritans who were escaping the excesses and tyranny of the Church of England and the British Parliament. In 1630 Roger Williams (ca. 1603–1683), a charismatic Puritan minister, and his family arrived in the Massachusetts Bay Colony. He discovered that the Boston church was under colonial government control, so he refused a post there and settled instead in Salem, a community north of Boston, where he worked as a minister. Williams was an outspoken critic of colony authorities, often accusing them of abusing their powers. In 1635 the general court of the Massachusetts Bay Colony, fearing his views would spread and corrupt others, banished him from the colony.

Williams fled into the wilderness in the middle of winter rather than risk being sent to prison in England. With the help of the local Indians, Williams survived the harsh winter, eventually traveling south and arriving in the area known today as the state of Rhode Island. He bought land from the natives who lived there, named it Providence, and invited his family and friends from Salem to join him in creating a new settlement, outside the control of the Massachusetts Bay Colony.

Williams's next move was truly revolutionary. He drafted a document of governance that transferred his personal ownership of Providence to a communal ownership by all the settlers of Providence and in that document he made no mention of God, which was unheard of in the Western world at that time. Williams thus created the first separation of church and state. Although he was a man of deep piety who believed that God was involved in every aspect of life, he also believed that the purity of religion necessitated that civil governance be separated from the church. This radical concept became a primary feature of the US Constitution 140 years later, protecting the church from state intrusion via the First Amendment's establishment clause: "Congress shall make no law respecting an establishment of religion."

Williams's travails, however, were not yet over. Massachusetts Bay Colony forces took over Providence, and Williams sailed to England in 1643 to ask Parliament for a colony charter so that Providence could operate independently. In an effort to support his case, Williams published a pamphlet in February 1644 that outlined the hypocrisy of the Puritan colony escaping political and religious tyranny in England only to establish a state-controlled church in the New World that did not permit the establishment of any other church. Williams argued in favor of a charter for his Rhode Island settlement as an experiment in what he called "soul liberty," which closely aligns with the modern concept of religious liberty or freedom of conscience. Even though Williams had a devoted following, his ideas were not generally popular. Nevertheless, his pleas for treating the Rhode Island settlement as a distant experiment were heard—perhaps in part to get him and his followers to leave England—and Parliament granted Williams his charter in March 1644.

Williams returned to Providence and lived a full and long life, passing away at the age of eighty. Sixty years later Thomas Jefferson (1743–1826) was born. Just eight years after Jefferson's birth, James Madison (1751–1836) was born. These men would eventually encode Williams's revolutionary ideas of religious liberty and separation of church and state into the US Constitution. Compared with Europe, where rulers were granted their power by the will of God, and government and religion were always closely and purposefully entwined, the idea that government would not dictate how the church operated and the church would not dictate to government was truly innovative.

In the early twenty-first century, Americans are still debating the separation of church and state and how to apply it to life today. The authors in *Opposing Viewpoints: Religious Liberty* debate the many facets of this issue under the following chapter titles: "Why Is Religious Liberty Important and Controversial?," "What Does the US Constitution Say About Religious Liberty?," "Is Religious Liberty Under Threat?," and "What Is the Impact of Politics on Religious Liberty?" Addressing these questions reveals the key role religious liberty plays in modern life and its importance for people all over the world.

CHAPTER 1

Why Is Religious Liberty Important and Controversial?

Chapter Preface

Religious liberty touches on deeply held and very personal beliefs. Religious beliefs are often handed down through generations of families or are hard-won through personal experience and self-reflection; thus religion can make up a significant aspect of a person's identity, whether the person is religious, agnostic (believes it is impossible to know whether God exists), or atheistic (does not believe God exists). The framers of the US Constitution made religious liberty a political priority, setting forth the establishment clause and the free-exercise clause in the First Amendment of the Constitution. They also described religious liberty as an inalienable right, meaning that this freedom is automatically granted to all people and cannot be taken away—although it can be infringed upon. The framers' position on religious liberty as an inalienable right set an important worldwide precedent.

Given the intimate nature of religion, people understandably have strong emotional reactions to the issue of religious liberty. Violence over religious liberty is endemic in many parts of the world, such as China and Egypt, but in the United States it is debated in courts, in Congress, in the media, on social networks, and across dinner tables. The free-exercise clause of the First Amendment makes safe debate possible. The establishment clause does not grant religious liberty to individuals—the framers recognized that they do not need to codify freedom of religion because it is an inalienable right—instead the establishment clause bars the federal government from establishing a state religion.

Religion is a moral guide for many people, although humanists argue that morality does not belong solely to religion and that atheists are just as capable of knowing right from wrong. In the best light, religious liberty provides freedom to all people to execute their beliefs in reasonable fashion without fear of reprisal; however, interpretations of how to apply religious liberty in contemporary life differ, leading to conflict over free expression and discrimination. The authors of the viewpoints in this chapter debate why religious liberty is important, as well as controversial.

> "*The American Founders frequently stated that virtue and religion are essential to maintaining a free society.*"

Religious Liberty Is Essential to Ensure a Free Society

Jennifer A. Marshall

In the following viewpoint, Jennifer A. Marshall argues that religious liberty is an inherent right handed down by God. She maintains that religious expression is not supposed to be kept out of the public sector because that repression of expression goes against the inalienable right of religious liberty. Marshall further contends that religion engenders moral behavior and thus is beneficial to communities and government. She concludes that the United States can best support worldwide religious freedom by standing as a good example itself. Jennifer A. Marshall is a director at the Heritage Foundation, a conservative public policy research organization in Washington, DC.

As you read, consider the following questions:

1. According to Marshall, what percentage of Americans are members of a local religious congregation?

2. Where does the phrase "separation of church and state" originate, and who wrote it, according to Marshall?

3. What correlation does the author draw between religious freedom and economics?

Religious liberty and a thriving religious culture are defining attributes of the United States, characterizing the American order as much as its political system and market economy. From the earliest settlements of the 17th century to the great social reform causes led by religious congregations in the late 19th century and again in the 20th century, religion has been a dominant theme of American life.

Today [in 2010], almost 90 percent of Americans say that religion is at least "somewhat important" in their lives. About 60 percent are members of a local religious congregation. Faith-based organizations are extremely active in providing for social needs at home and in sending aid abroad.

Why does religious liberty matter—to America and to the world?

A Cornerstone of American Life

Freedom of religion is a cornerstone of the American experiment. That is because religious faith is not merely a matter of "toleration" but is understood to be the exercise of "inherent natural rights." As [US president] George Washington once observed: "[T]he Government of the United States, which gives to bigotry no sanction, to persecution no assistance, requires only that they who live under its protection should demean themselves [i.e., conduct themselves] as good citizens in giving it on all occasions their effectual support." And "what is here a right towards men, is a duty towards the Creator," [founding father and future president] James Madison wrote in his [1785 paper] Memorial and Remonstrance [Against Reli-

gious Assessments]. "This duty is precedent, both in order of time and in degree of obligation, to the claims of Civil Society."

The model of religious liberty brilliantly designed by Madison and the other American Founders is central to the success of the American experiment. It is essential to America's continued pursuit of the ideals stated in the Declaration of Independence, the ordered liberty embodied in the Constitution, and peace and stability around the world.

The key to America's religious liberty success story is its constitutional order. The Founders argued that virtue derived from religion is indispensable to limited government. The Constitution therefore guaranteed religious free exercise while prohibiting the establishment of a national religion. This Constitutional order produced a constructive relationship between religion and state that balances citizens' dual allegiances to God and earthly authorities without forcing believers to abandon (or moderate) their primary loyalty to God.

This reconciling of civil and religious authorities, and the creation of a Constitutional order that gave freedom to competing religious groups, helped develop a popular spirit of self-government. All the while, religious congregations, family, and other private associations exercise moral authority that is essential to maintaining limited government. The American Founders frequently stated that virtue and religion are essential to maintaining a free society because they preserve "the moral conditions of freedom."

Religion and the Public Sector

Today, the religious roots of the American order and the role of religion in its continued success are poorly understood. One source of the confusion is the phrase "separation of church and state," a phrase used by President Thomas Jefferson in a widely misunderstood letter to the Danbury Baptist Association of Connecticut in 1802. Many think this means a radical separation of religion and politics. Some have gone so far as to suggest that religion should be entirely personal and private, kept out of public life and institutions like public schools.

That is incorrect: Jefferson wanted to protect states' freedom of religion from federal government control and religious groups' freedom to tend to their internal matters of faith and practice without government interference generally. Unfortunately, Jefferson's phrase is probably more widely known than the actual text of the Constitution's First Amendment: "Congress shall make no law respecting an establishment of religion, or prohibiting the free exercise thereof."

The American model of religious liberty takes a strongly positive view of religious practice, both private and public. While it does not mean that anything and everything done in the name of religious liberty is not subject to the rule of law, it does mean that the law ought to make as much room as possible for the practice of religious faith. Far from privatizing religion, it assumes that religious believers and institutions will take active roles in society, including engaging in politics and policy-making and helping form the public's moral consensus. In fact, the American Founders considered religious engagement in shaping the public morality essential to ordered liberty and the success of their experiment in self-government.

Granted by the Creator

Defying predictions that political and social progress would eventually marginalize religion, religious belief and practice remain widespread and vibrant around the world.

"The very things that were supposed to destroy religion—democracy and markets, technology and reason—are combining to make it stronger," write the authors of a book about religion's persistence in culture and politics around the world [*God Is Back: How the Global Revival of Faith Is Changing the World*].

In this era—as in all prior human history—God has occupied the thoughts of man. Conscience, the mystery of existence, and the prospect of death challenge every human being to grapple with questions of transcendence and divine reality.

Religious freedom recognizes the right of all people to pursue these transcendent ends. This right is granted not by government but by the Creator. By respecting it, a government acknowledges that such ultimate issues are outside its jurisdiction, and that conscience is answerable to a higher authority than the law of the land. Individuals and institutions should be free to believe and to act in response to divine reality.

Because religious liberty is the bedrock for all human freedom, it provides a sturdy foundation for limited government. Liberty of conscience demands, and ultimately justifies, limited government.

Conversely, limited government requires individual responsibility. Freedom engages the moral responsibility of each and every person. In a free society, religion is an ally of good government as it forms the moral character of individuals and communities.

Religious Freedom and Respect

Religious freedom is a fundamental human right that ought to be enjoyed by the people of all nations. This principle has been recognized in the 1948 Universal Declaration of Human Rights and subsequent international agreements. Despite widespread recognition, many people are unable to exercise this basic liberty.

Even with religion's global prevalence, religious freedom is far from universally respected. About a third of the world's nations restrict religion to a high or very high degree, according to the Pew Forum on Religion & Public Life. Seventy percent of the world's population lives in these countries.

In some cases, totalitarian governments have oppressed religious individuals and groups generally. In others, statist regimes built on an established religion have persecuted religious minorities.

Countries designated by the U.S. State Department as "countries of particular concern" because they restrict religious freedom (such as North Korea, Iran, and Burma [now known as Myanmar]) suffer in other ways as well. They also tend to have the least economic liberty—and some of the worst economic outcomes.

On the other hand, governments that respect religious liberty tend to respect other freedoms as well. Religious freedom is strongly related to political liberty, economic freedom, and prosperity. As one researcher of international religious liberty notes, "[W]herever religious freedom is high, there tends to be fewer incidents of armed conflict, better health outcomes, higher levels of earned income, and better educational opportunities for women."

Public and Private Religious Expression

The 1998 International Religious Freedom Act made religious liberty an official part of U.S. foreign policy. The United States committed to promote freedom of religion as "a fundamental human right and as a source of stability for all countries" and to "identify and denounce regimes" that engage in persecution on the basis of religion.

Condemning and curtailing religious persecution is a critical goal, but religious freedom includes much more. Our vision of religious liberty must be robust.

Attempts to relegate religion to private life or to prevent religious institutions from conducting their business according to their beliefs threaten this fundamental freedom. Religious

Government Restrictions on Religion Affect the Majority of People in the World

The percentage of the world's countries with high or very high government restrictions is about 20% . . .

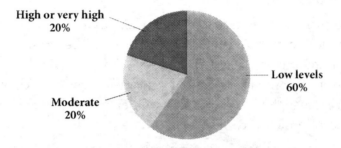

High or very high
20%

Moderate
20%

Low levels
60%

. . . but because many of these are populous countries, the percentage of the world's population living with high or very high government restrictions is 57%.

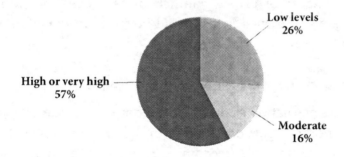

Low levels
26%

High or very high
57%

Moderate
16%

Note: Totals may not add up to 100% due to rounding.

TAKEN FROM: "Global Restrictions on Religion," Pew Forum on Religion and Public Life, December 2009, p. 8.

individuals and institutions should be free to exercise their religious belief within their private spheres as well as to engage publicly on the basis of religion. Believers should be free to persuade others to embrace their beliefs. Individuals should be able to leave or change their religion without fear of reprisal, and all should have the right to protection under the rule of law regardless of belief.

A Model for All

The most secure and consistent protection for religious liberty needs to be rooted in constitutional government. U.S. public diplomacy can support the development of such robust religious freedom by telling America's success story.

That requires that U.S. policymakers understand and be able to articulate the role of religion in the American constitutional order. In the 21st-century war of ideas, U.S. public diplomacy must rely on the bedrock of American founding principles in the fight against potent ideologies that present strong, coherent, and deeply misguided explanations of the nature and purpose of human existence. Evaluating religious dynamics around the world should become a regular function of analysis, and articulating the role of religion in the U.S. should be a consistent feature of communications strategy.

Religion and traditional morality continue to play a significant role in American public life. Most Americans continue to attach great significance to religious faith and practice, marriage, family, and raising children in a morally rich and supportive environment—values shared in many highly religious societies around the world.

Religious freedom is the birthright of all people, but too few governments around the world acknowledge it and far too many people have never enjoyed it.

One of the gifts of providence to the United States is a Constitution that has successfully safeguarded this fundamental right. It is a gift Americans should cherish and a model for all throughout the world.

"[The Christian Right is] waging a multi-pronged battle against LGBT rights . . . on the premise that equality for gays restricts the religious liberty of Christians to discriminate against them."

The "Religious Liberty" Bullies and Their Fight Against LGBT Equality

Jay Michaelson

In the following viewpoint, Jay Michaelson argues that the goal of religious-liberty advocates is to legalize discrimination. He maintains that this strategy has resulted in some success for the Christian right in establishing state-sanctioned legal barriers to same-sex marriage, birth control, abortion, and other personal matters. Michaelson concludes that a balance can be found but that the fight for civil rights in the United States is not over yet. Jay Michaelson is an author and an associated editor for the Daily Beast website.

As you read, consider the following questions:

1. According to Michaelson, how many states have laws that permit an employer to fire an employee for being gay?

2. What religious group has joined evangelical Christians in the fight for religious liberty, according to the author?

3. Why does Michaelson argue that health insurance is not something an employer can opt out of for reasons of conscience?

Thirty-five years ago [in 1978], having lost the moral battle for segregation, a small group of evangelicals met to re-think their attitude toward politics. Unlike Catholics and mainline Protestants, evangelicals had tended to stay out of secular politics, believing it to be irredeemable. But with the IRS's [Internal Revenue Service] decision to withdraw tax-exempt status from the evangelical Bob Jones University, which discriminated against African-Americans, the Christian right was born. Their mission, they said, was to defend "religious liberty."

Fighting for the Right to Discriminate

Today [in 2013] is a different age—but the players, and the rhetoric, are the same. Today a far-right coalition of conserva-tive Catholics and evangelicals perceive that they have lost the moral battle against LGBT [lesbian, gay, bisexual, and trans-gender] equality, particularly same-sex marriage. And so, as described in a lengthy report released [in March 2013] by the think tank Political Research Associates and chiefly authored by this writer, they are waging a multi-pronged battle against LGBT rights, not on substantive moral grounds but on the premise that equality for gays restricts the religious liberty of Christians to discriminate against them.

Of course, this is rhetoric, not reality. Forty years ago, the newly minted Christian right "played the victim" by claiming that a racist school, rather than the students being discriminated against, was the true victim. And today religious-liberty activists claim that bullies are the real victims because they cannot "express their views about homosexuality." They claim that businesses who say "No Gays Allowed" are being oppressed because they are forced to "facilitate" gay marriages. And they claim that the real targets of discrimination are not gay people, who in 24 states can be fired from their jobs simply for being gay, but employers who can't fire them.

Yet unlike recent anti-gay sloganeering, the religious-liberty campaign makes use not of theological arguments but of civil libertarian ones, and as such is much harder to recognize than the usual Bible-quoting bigotry. Indeed, Catholic-funded organizations such as The Becket Fund—named, not coincidentally, for the archbishop who chose martyrdom rather than obedience to the secular law—and the U.S. Conference of Catholic Bishops have co-opted the work of respected law professors such as Douglas Laycock of Virginia. They have even convinced Stanford University to establish a Becket-funded "Center for Religious Liberty."

"Religious Liberty" Is a Code Word

The notion that anti-discrimination law offends religious liberty has even found its way to the very top of our political life. At the vice presidential debate last fall, Rep. Paul Ryan accused the [Barack] Obama administration of "assaulting the religious liberties of Catholic charities, Catholic churches, Catholic hospitals." But all churches and most hospitals are already exempt from anti-discrimination law and need not provide reproductive health services either, despite receiving enormous government subsidies.

Religious liberty is a code word, like family values. Though Laycock and other academics may be sincere, the Family Re-

A License to Discriminate

Organizations such as the Family Research Council and the Liberty Institute insist that the First Amendment gives people a license to use religion to discriminate against others. By this logic, people also have a right to discriminate against someone because they are Jewish, because they are African American, or because they are a woman, as long as there is a "religious freedom" rationale behind doing so.

Crosby Burns,
Center for American Progress, October 15, 2012.

search Council, Christian Legal Society, Ethics and Public Policy Institute, and the legion of other Christian right organizations are chasing the same bugaboos as ever—gay rights, abortion, prayer-free schools—and simply repurposing an old, racist rhetoric to fight the same social battles as always.

(Not all religious-liberty activists are Christians; a handful of Orthodox Jews have joined the campaign, providing a Jewish fig leaf for an otherwise hard-right theocratic Christian movement.)

This strategy has worked. Several states include religious exemptions to nondiscrimination law and same-sex marriage laws. "Conscience clauses" have limited women's access to reproductive health for decades. And, in the highest-profile religious-liberty campaign of recent years, right-wing activists won significant new exemptions to Obamacare's requirement that employers provide health insurance to their employees. Now not only churches but any church-affiliated organization—those aforementioned Catholic hospitals, for example—need not provide coverage for contraception.

Businesses and Employee Health Care

But that's not enough, not by a long shot. The Becket Fund has recently filed 37 lawsuits, all around the country, seeking to extend the exemption to *any* employer who feels religiously aggrieved by providing health insurance coverage that some employee might someday use to obtain contraception. From the hysterical op-eds [opinion/editorials] written by one of Becket's clients, you would think that the CEO [chief executive officer] is personally performing an abortion. The truth, as the Supreme Court held, is that health insurance is now a kind of tax. And just as a pacifist can't opt out of paying taxes used for war, so too a religious employer can't opt out of these taxes because an employee might use them for a form of health care with which the employer disagrees.

Besides, this is a slippery slope. Suppose a business is owned by Christian Scientists, who object to many forms of modern medicine. Should that business's employees be deprived of health insurance entirely?

Or suppose a Christian business owner dislikes Jews as much as she dislikes gays. Not just dislikes—suppose she holds all Jews responsible for the death of Jesus Christ. Should such a business owner be able to post "No Jews Allowed," like the wedding photographer who refused to photograph a gay couple?

Playing by the Same Rules

Of course not. Religious-liberty rhetoric notwithstanding, civil rights is always about balancing competing interests. If the wedding photographer refuses to take a picture of a gay couple, the gay couple suffers injustice. If the wedding photographer must obey the same anti-discrimination laws as everyone else, then he or she has to put up with it, because this is America, and America doesn't believe in discrimination.

Fortunately, this is a religious value as well. Christianity believes in rendering unto Caesar what is Caesar's, and God what is God's. Corporations do not have consciences; they are commercial entities well within Caesar's domain. You want to be in the marketplace, you play by the same rules as everyone else.

Unfortunately, such points are lost in the din of right-wing talk radio. Just last fall in Minnesota, for example, the religious-liberty crowd was warning that if same-sex marriage passed, ministers would be compelled to perform gay weddings. This was an out-and-out lie, and they knew it. No rabbi can be forced to perform an intermarriage [between a Jew and a Gentile]. No Catholic priest can be forced to marry two divorcees. And no, Virginia, no minister could ever be forced to solemnize a gay wedding, a straight wedding, or any other kind of wedding she or he found objectionable. But try telling that to honest Christians who are being robocalled on the eve of an election.

Religious liberty is being used to mask a conservative Christian agenda—the same agenda that's been pushed for half a century now. Some on the far right may sincerely believe their liberties are being threatened, but they believed that about desegregation too. A belief does not make something so. The question is how many new believers they'll recruit before this crusade is defeated.

> "Those who advocate strong conscience
> protections—whether from a contra-
> ceptive mandate or from federal recog-
> nition of same-sex marriage—do so
> sincerely."

In Defense of Religious Liberty

Ken Blackwell

In the following viewpoint, Ken Blackwell directly refutes Jay Michaelson's viewpoint. Blackwell disputes Michaelson's claims that same-sex marriage can be equated with racial equality and that there is a right-wing agenda being served by the opposition to same-sex marriage. Blackwell concludes that Michaelson's viewpoint is unfair and ineffective and is an attempt to shut down dissent. Ken Blackwell is the senior fellow for family empowerment at the Family Research Council, a conservative Christian group that promotes traditional family values.

As you read, consider the following questions:

1. According to Blackwell, how does the fight for racial equality differ from the fight to support same-sex marriage?

2. What trick does the author employ to impress upon readers that those who oppose same-sex marriage are not the same as racists?

3. Why does Blackwell disagree with Michaelson about the existence of a right-wing agenda?

Recently, Jay Michaelson wrote a piece for *The Daily Beast* titled "The 'Religious Liberty' Bullies and Their Fight Against LGBT Equality." In it, he suggests that those who oppose same-sex marriage for religious reasons are the same as the racists who opposed desegregation laws. He calls those who protect religious liberty, and who therefore are willing to stick up for the rights of religious people who oppose same-sex marriage, insincere and "racist," as well. "Today is a different age—but the players, and the rhetoric, are the same," he states. Later on, he says that defenders of religious liberty are "simply repurposing an old, racist rhetoric to fight the same social battles as always."

There are three points to be made here.

One, there can be no comparison between the fight for racial equality and the movement for same-sex marriage. Two, supporting the traditional definition of marriage is not the same (or even akin) to supporting institutionalized racism. Three, concerns about religious liberty are both sincere and valid, especially regarding the social trends Michaelson discusses in both his article and a related report he recently released.

My first point is that there can be no comparison between the fight for racial equality and the movement supporting same-sex marriage. To begin with, race occupies a singular place in our country's history and laws. Our country fought a bloody Civil War and passed three separate Constitutional Amendments to rid our society of the injustice that was slavery. The segregation laws that followed were ugly remnants of a culture of racial slavery, and they were immoral and unjust. They defied the American promise "that all men are created equal, that they are endowed by their Creator with certain unalienable Rights, that among these are Life, Liberty and the pursuit of Happiness." Black Americans were enslaved, literally deprived of their liberty, often robbed of life, and denied the opportunity to pursue happiness. Segregation laws were a legal statement of inequality. No other law in American history spells indignity and injustice like they did, and no other law so explicitly rings false to our country's founding principles.

Now, for the second point.

Applying the racism of segregation-era America to today's "social battles" does not make for a compelling comparison. To state what should be obvious, not all racists oppose same-sex marriage, and not all who oppose same-sex marriage are racists. To say otherwise is disrespectful and frankly ludicrous. No reasonable person is advocating "segregation" between the opposite-sex attracted population and the same-sex attracted population. I don't need to go into detail on this point. It should be enough for readers to simply think of their own family, friends, and acquaintances—some of whom, no doubt, are uncertain about or against same-sex marriage—and realize that pairing "racist" with "opposed to same-sex marriage" means labeling many reasonable people as outright bigots. That kind of accusation has heavy consequences and is dangerous to healthy discourse.

Marriage, as it stands and has stood for centuries, is not an institution that was driven into existence by bigotry, or constructed to deny some right to same-sex partners. People who oppose same-sex marriage do so for a variety of reasons. There are many who oppose same-sex marriage for religious reasons, and others for reasons grounded in history, philosophy, and our country's Constitution. What traditional marriage supporters generally want, is to uphold a centuries-old definition of marriage as between one man and one woman.

It is a fixed definition. They see marriage as unique and un-changing, valuable because of (and contingent on) its singular male-female union, and meaningless without it.

My third point refers to the idea that those who are con-cerned about religious liberty rights in and around same-sex marriage are covertly advancing some right-wing agenda. This is misleading, false, and insulting. Religious liberty is a real, fundamental right, first in our Constitutional Amendments. It's what allows a man to be a conscientious objector, or a church to choose its own minister. In general, it's what pro-tects religious people who hold views that are out of political favor. Michaelson admits that intellectuals and politicians on both ends of the political spectrum support religious liberty. He simply thinks that religious liberty is much more limited than it is or ever has been.

As the recent (large) batch of cases against the Health and Human Services contraceptive mandate demonstrates, America has a diverse and principled religious population of citizens willing to fight for the right to express their faith in all aspects of life. That some, like Michaelson, don't agree that buying contraception for others violates a person's faith does not sud-denly appease the troubled consciences. Those who advocate strong conscience protections—whether from a contraceptive mandate or from federal recognition of same-sex mar-riage—do so sincerely.

We can all agree that the topic of same-sex marriage draws intense emotions from both sides. But those emotions do not justify branding people who disagree with us as liars or bigots. That's a cheap way to silence dissenters, when there is real and substantive debate to be had. It's also a grave insult to honest, truth-seeking individuals, and a violation of the principles of American society. All people should be free to explore and de-fine their beliefs. And all should be free to speak, act, vote and advocate according to their beliefs.

"Religious freedom is a fundamental natural right and first among our civil liberties."

The United States Was Founded on Religious Liberty

Charles J. Chaput

In the following viewpoint, Charles J. Chaput (pronounced "chap-you") argues that religious liberty is a fundamental right protected by the US Constitution and not just personal bias but part of human nature. He points out that the right to worship is only part of the inalienable right to religious liberty. Chaput concludes that religious freedom is under serious attack in the United States and that current leaders have strayed from the intention of the Founders. Charles J. Chaput is an author and the Roman Catholic archbishop of Philadelphia, Pennsylvania. Chaput's viewpoint is adapted from his testimony submitted to the United States Commission on Civil Rights.

As you read, consider the following questions:

1. According to Chaput, what three elements make up the model of public life in the United States?

2. What significant legal victory did advocates of religious liberty win in 2012, according to the author?

3. Why does Chaput argue that religious belief should not be redefined as a type of private bias?

My remarks today are purely my own. But they're shaped by twenty-five years as a Catholic bishop and the social and religious ministries that such work involves; ministries that serve not just Catholics, but the much larger public and common good.

I also served for three years as a commissioner with the United States Commission on International Religious Freedom. That experience confirmed for me the unique role that religious faith, religious believers, and religious communities play in genuine human development. It also taught me the importance of religious liberty both abroad and in our own country.

Simply put, religious freedom is a fundamental natural right and first among our civil liberties. And I believe this fact is borne out by the priority protection it specifically enjoys, along with freedom of expression, in the Constitution's First Amendment.

I'd like to make four brief points.

Religion Matters

Here's my first point: *Religious faith and practice are cornerstones of the American experience.* It's worth recalling that James Madison, John Adams, John Carroll, John Jay, George Washington, Alexander Hamilton, Benjamin Franklin, Thomas Jefferson—in fact, nearly all the American Founders—saw religious faith as vital to the life of a free people. They believed that liberty and happiness grow organically out of virtue. And virtue needs grounding in religious faith.

To put it another way: At the heart of the American model of public life is an essentially religious vision of man, government, and God. This model has given us a free, open, and non-sectarian society marked by an astonishing variety of cultural and religious expressions. But our system's success does not result from the procedural mechanisms our Founders put in place. Our system works *precisely* because of the moral assumptions that undergird it. And those moral assumptions have a *religious* grounding.

When the Founders talked about religion, they meant something much more demanding than a vague "spirituality." The distinguished legal scholar Harold Berman showed that the Founders—though they had differing views about religious faith among themselves—understood religion positively as "both belief in God and belief in an after-life of reward for virtue, and punishment for sin." In other words, religion *mattered*—personally and socially. It was more than a private preference. It made people live differently and live better. And therefore people's faith was assumed to have broad implications, including the social, economic, and political kind.

Faith Requires Community

That leads to my second point: *Freedom of religion is more than freedom of worship.* The right to worship is a necessary but not a sufficient part of religious liberty. For most religious believers, and certainly for Christians, faith requires community. It begins in worship, but it also demands preaching, teaching, and service; in other words, active engagement with society. Faith is always personal but never private. And it involves more than prayer at home and Mass on Sunday—although these things are vitally important. Real faith always bears fruit in public witness and public action. Otherwise it's just empty words.

The Founders saw the value of publicly engaged religious faith because they inherited its legacy and experienced its formative influence themselves. They created a nation designed

Religion in America

The American model of religious liberty and its thriving religious culture are defining attributes of the United States. These features characterize the American order as much as its democratic political system and market economy. Religion has been a dominant theme from the earliest settlements to the great social justice causes led by religious congregations in the late 19th century and again in the 20th century. Today [2009], almost 90 percent of Americans say that religion is at least "somewhat important" in their lives. About 60 percent are members of a local religious congregation. Faith-based organizations are extremely active in providing for social needs at home and in sending aid abroad.

Jennifer A. Marshall,
Heritage Foundation report, January 15, 2009.

in advance to depend on the moral convictions of religious believers, and to welcome their active role in public life.

Real Threats to Religious Liberty

Here's my third point: *Threats against religious freedom in our country are not imaginary or overstated. They're happening right now. They're immediate, serious, and real.* Last year [2012], religious liberty advocates won a significant and appropriate Supreme Court victory in the 9–0 *Hosanna-Tabor v. EEOC* decision[1] But what was stunning even to the justices in that case was the disregard for traditional constitutional un-

---

1. The Equal Employment Opportunity Commission (EEOC) sued Hosanna-Tabor Evangelical Lutheran Church and School for illegally firing a teacher. The school argued that the government did not have a right to interfere in the relationship between a religious institution and one of its ministers. The high court agreed.

derstandings of religious freedom shown by the government's arguments against the Lutheran church and school.

Hosanna-Tabor is not an isolated case. It belongs to a pattern of government coercion that includes the current administration's HHS [Department of Health and Human Services] mandate [requiring, under the Affordable Care Act of 2010, that employers provide health care for their employees that includes contraception], which violates the religious identity and mission of many religiously affiliated or inspired public ministries; interfering with the conscience rights of medical providers, private employers, and individual citizens; and attacks on the policies, hiring practices, and tax statuses of religious charities and ministries.

Why is this hostility happening? I believe much of it links to Catholic and other religious teaching on the dignity of life and human sexuality. Catholic moral convictions about abortion, contraception, the purpose of sexuality, and the nature of marriage are rooted not just in revelation, but also in reason and natural law. Human beings have a nature that's not just the product of accident or culture, but inherent, universal, and rooted in permanent truths knowable to reason.

This understanding of the human person is the grounding of the entire American experiment. If human nature is not much more than modeling clay, and no permanent human nature exists by the hand of the Creator, then natural, unalienable rights obviously can't exist. And no human "rights" can finally claim priority over the interests of the state.

An Expression of Subjective Beliefs

The problem, as law scholar Gerard Bradley points out, is that critics of religious faith tend to reduce all of these moral convictions to an expression of subjective beliefs. And if they're purely subjective beliefs, then—so the critics argue—they can't be rationally defended. And because they're rationally indefensible, they should be treated as a form of prejudice. In effect, two thousand years of moral experience, moral reasoning, and religious conviction become a species of bias. And arguing against same-sex "marriage" thus amounts to religiously blessed homophobia.

There's more, though. When religious belief is redefined downward to a kind of private bias, then the religious identity of institutional ministries has no public value—other than the utility of getting credulous people to do good things. So exempting Catholic adoption agencies, for example, from placing children with gay couples becomes a concession to private prejudice. And concessions to private prejudice feed bigotry and hurt the public. Or so the reasoning goes. This is how moral teaching and religious belief end up being branded as hate speech.

Here's my fourth and final point: From the beginning, believers—alone and in communities—have shaped American history simply by trying to live their faith in the world. *We need to realize that America's founding documents assume an implicitly religious anthropology*—an idea of human nature, nature's God, and natural rights—that many of our leaders no longer really share.

We ignore that unhappy fact at our own expense.

*"Peace and creative living together in
our globalized and interconnected societies will be possible only if freedom of
religion is fully respected."*

Religious Liberty Promotes World Peace and Equity

Silvano M. Tomasi

*In the following viewpoint, Silvano M. Tomasi contends that re-
ligious liberty for people of all religions and for people who do
not believe in any religion is the key to peaceful coexistence. He
concludes that the American experiment in religious liberty is
groundbreaking and stands as an example for how other nations
can legislate to protect religious liberty. Silvano M. Tomasi is the
titular archbishop of Cercina, Italy, and the Vatican's permanent
observer to the United Nations.*

As you read, consider the following questions:

1. According to Tomasi, what percentage of the world's
   population lives in countries where government restrictions on or social hostilities toward religion have actually declined?

2. What does the author claim is the American contribution to the Second Vatican Council?

3. What is the connection between world peace and religious liberty, according to Tomasi?

At present, there is no doubt that religious freedom is under stress worldwide. During the 20th century, some forty-five million Christians died because of their faith. The trend continues. A 2011 study on global restrictions on religion by the Pew Research Center's Forum on Religion & Public Life found that 70% of the world's population lives in countries with high restrictions on religious beliefs and practices, the brunt of which often falls on religious minorities—including, in some cases, people who are secular or nonreligious. Additionally, more than 2.2 billion people, nearly a third (32%) of the world's total population, live in countries where either government restrictions on religion or social hostilities involving religion rose substantially between mid-2006 and mid-2009. Only 1% of the world's population lives in countries where government restrictions or social hostilities have declined. The number of countries in which governments used at least some measure of force against religious groups or individuals rose from 91 (46%) in the period ending in mid-2008 to 101 (51%) in the period ending in mid-2009. The consequent violence was wide-ranging, including murder, physical abuse, imprisonment, detention or displacement from one's home, as well as damage to or destruction of personal or religious properties. On the increase are mob violence, religious-motivated terrorist groups and the commission of malicious acts by private citizens and groups motivated by religious hatred. Christians are the first target.

Laws Meant to Protect Actually Punish

The Pew Report adds that restrictions on religion are particularly common in the 59 countries that prohibit blasphemy, apostasy [giving up one's religion] or defamation of religion. While such laws are sometimes promoted as a way to protect religion, in practice they often serve to punish religious minorities whose beliefs are deemed unorthodox or heretical. A simple review of the daily press confirms the Pew study: bombs are exploded in churches during Mass in Nigeria and Kenya; threats are carried out against the ancient Christian communities of Iraq, and now of Syria, thus forcing them into exile; a Christian girl of 11, living with Down Syndrome, Rimsha Masih, is arrested on charges of blasphemy and put in jail in Pakistan, for purportedly burning pages of the Koran and 400 Christian families of her poor neighborhood took flight in fear for their lives; Sufi shrines are turned to rubble in Libya; a rabbi is attacked in the streets of Berlin [Germany] and has to be hospitalized and rabbinical [Jewish] students are advised not to wear their kippa [skull cap, also called a yarmulke] in public places; a Catholic Bishop Ma Da Qin is placed under home arrest for allegiance to the Pope; Christians are in flight from Northern Mali [in Africa] to escape the violent attacks of [Muslim] fundamentalists. The International Society for Human Rights estimates that 80 percent of all acts of religious discrimination in the world today are directed at Christians and that some 150,000 Christian are killed for the faith every year. . . .

The Teachings of the Church

The importance of religious freedom for promotion of the common good and peaceful coexistence also has become a major chapter in the social doctrine of the Church. There is a convergence of language and substance between international human rights developments and Church teaching. Besides, the educational role of the Church has helped in no small way the consolidation of democratic institutions. The American contribution to the Second Vatican Council opened the door wide for an understanding of religious freedom that truly universalizes this right: "This Vatican Council declares that the human person has a right to religious freedom. This freedom means that all men are to be immune from coercion on the part of individuals or of social groups and of any human power, in such wise that no one is to be forced to act in a manner contrary to his own beliefs, whether privately or publicly, whether alone or in association with others, within due limits. The Council further declares that the right to religious freedom has its foundation in the very dignity of the human person as this dignity is known through the revealed word of God and by reason itself. This right of the human person to religious freedom is to be recognized in the constitutional law whereby society is governed and thus it is to become a civil right." The moral battle of Blessed John Paul II to sensitize the world's conscience that all believers should effectively enjoy religious freedom has led to the well-known results that transformed the map of Europe and global politics; his unique spiritual leadership advanced freedom in the world. The aspiration for religious freedom also has been at the root of recent democratic movements that led to the fall of several dicatorships.

Religious Liberty and World Peace

Through the masterful addresses of Our Holy Father Benedict XVI and, in line with him, through his Representatives in the U.N. arena, the voice of the Holy See reminds the international community that, even in our present circumstances, peace requires religious freedom. In fact, the promotion of full and universal respect for this liberty guides the activity of the Holy See in international and intergovernmental organizations, in the stipulation of concordats and other agreements, and in the service of its diplomatic corps. The commitment that flows from faith benefits the entire society. The example of Mother Teresa of Calcutta offers clear evidence.

Profound changes have taken place in most societies, however, due to an increasing differentiation of beliefs, life styles, cultural traditions, ethnic identities, secularization and extreme individualism. Globalization forces us to interact across national, cultural, religious and other boundaries. Democratic States are challenged to search for common acceptable criteria to preserve social peace and cohesion. Certainly the ethical core of fundamental convictions within each person must be respected, protected and guaranteed; if need be, through an affirmative action by public authorities. But such an individualized focus on belief might also facilitate legitimation of behaviours, or mere passions, that are quite distant from the lived and institutional dimensions of religions. This religion *à la carte* places the legislator in a difficult situation that risks the limitation of religious freedom in an effort to find pragmatic solutions. God's existence, the assumption in all the historical journey in the development of the doctrine of religious liberty, is no longer assumed. Nor is the anthropological foundation of human rights preserved.

Finding Common Values

The question then arises of how to find common values to keep cohesion and peaceful coexistence in society, while respecting religious freedom in the new circumstances. In common we have our human nature; this becomes the starting point for the search. Nature, reason and the profound desire of the human heart for fulfilment provide the possibility to discover and understand the basic core values of every person. "Any well-regulated and productive association of men in society demands the acceptance of one fundamental principle: that each individual man is truly a person." wrote Pope John XXIII. "His is a nature, that is, endowed with intelligence and free will. As such he has rights and duties, which together flow as a direct consequence from his nature. These rights and duties are universal and inviolable, and therefore altogether inalienable." In this line of reasoning, freedom is not separated from truth, and thus eventual and objective ethical limits to personal and social conduct are implied. The range of freedom of the person, while she finds limits in her reference to truth, extends beyond the subjective dimension. The person does not arrive to be a person without relations to others.

Reasonable for the Common Good

Therefore freedom of religion includes a communitarian and institutional aspect, as well as *inter alia* [among other things] the right of each religion to establish its own rules, to exercise the power of self-organization and to disseminate its doctrine. The State cannot intrude on this process and can limit the exercise of institutional religious freedom only if such action is warranted in accord with the principles of respect for public order and the common good. Attempts by the State to restrict fundamental values, like the right to life, or to oblige a person to go against her conscience, can never be justified, since this would violate personal dignity and be detrimental to society itself. Moreover, compliance with certain core values provides a solid basis for social cohesion, respect for others and the well being of society as a whole. It has been aptly observed "that just as freedom of speech depends not only on one's right to say what's on one's mind, but on the existence of institutions like newspapers, universities, libraries, [political] parties, and associations, so freedom of religion also involves protecting the institutions that nourish individual free exercise."

Religious Liberty and Human Rights

A reasoned approach to human rights and religious liberty finds a universal appeal because it is centered on the person. But we cannot lose sight of the fact that the religious dimension of the person is part of human experience in all cultures and social contexts. The contribution of reason and of religious insights to support religious liberty is like the continuity of a ray of light that cannot be cut at any point. Instead of hostility, the correct relationship between religious norms and the public sphere can be articulated with reasonable arguments of a general character and without the exclusion of religious insights. From the mutual openness of believers of different religions and non-believers of good will, great benefits can derive for a dialogue among religions and convictions to promote peace and the common good of humanity as well as to establish a serene coexistence, social progress and institutional stability in each State. Indifference or an exclusive absorption in materialistic pursuits risks to relegate the fundamental right of religious freedom to be considered a "second class" right with the negative consequences of violent claims and insurgencies that the repression of this right has shown throughout history. Thus support of religious freedom calls for a culture of respect, for a system of education that teaches the value of searching together for the truth and of respect for the sincere beliefs of everyone, that encourages forgiveness and promotes harmony in a way that integral human development can truly be achieved.

Common Values Rooted in Human Nature

Pope John Paul II shared the learning from his personal experience when he taught that: "Dialogue between cultures, a privileged means for building the civilization of love, is based upon the recognition that *there are values which are common to all cultures* because they are rooted in the nature of the person. These values express humanity's most authentic and distinctive features. Leaving aside ideological prejudices and selfish interests, it is necessary to foster people's awareness of these shared values, in order to nurture that intrinsically universal cultural 'humus-soil' which makes for fruitful and constructive dialogue." A practical help to advance religious liberty in the world and its many derived benefits is the political monitoring of the implementation of this right that is undertaken by the European Union and by the U.S. State Depart-

Religious Liberty Promotes Stability

The denial of religious liberty by governments and private sectors around the world has serious implications for American national interests. As our own history has shown, religious freedom is necessary if democracy is to be peaceful and stable, yielding its benefits to all of its citizens. It is necessary if societies are to forestall the incubation and export of religious violence and extremism.

Thomas F. Farr, America, July 19, 2010.

ment, by the United Nations Human Rights Council's Universal Periodical Review of States, and in the annual Reports on how religious liberty fares in the countries of the world. Thus we note an increasing awareness of the link between foreign policy and religious freedom. Ultimately, each one of us should engage in this task. I am reminded of an old African story of the king lion escaping the forest in flames followed by all the animals. When the lion notices a tiny hummingbird flying counter current toward the fire he yells at him: "What do you think you are doing with your useless flight?" And the hummingbird replies: "I'm trying to put out the fire." Then the lion with a mocking laugh retorts: "With only one drop of water ... ?" Without breaking his flight the hummingbird answers: "I do my share."

The American Experiment

The novelty of the American experiment has been to guarantee the free exercise of religious liberty for individuals, for different religious groups, and for their religious-inspired institutions. This remains a lasting and valid contribution to the world. [American judge and author] John Noonan rightly de-

51

fined religious liberty as the "lustre" of the United States. Religious freedom was among the most relevant freedoms that gave origin and shape to the American colonies, then to the American states, and subsequently to the American Republic.

Americans have a special relationship with the value of religious liberty; it is well embedded, not just in their past, but also in their present. Our twentieth century Civil Rights movement was prompted by religious communities and personalities who substantially contributed to erase racial inequality.

But the special relationship between the United States and religious liberty has not been fruitful just for Americans. It has been fruitful for everybody. The American sensitivity to religious freedom played a prominent role in shaping the Universal Declaration of Human Rights. Thanks to the personal engagement of [First Lady] Eleanor Roosevelt . . . a deep understanding of religious freedom found its place in a foundational article of the Universal Declaration of Human rights. The American experience of religious freedom still is the focus of serious study in other parts of the world, including Europe. Scholars and legislators there still draw inspiration from American Constitutionalism when they try to find new and positive ways of conceiving the relationship between religions and the State. Even the Catholic Church learned much from the American experience as it shaped, during the Second Vatican Council, that which became the *Declaration on Religious Freedom*. The United States still plays a global role in upholding religious freedom as, in many ways, does the Church in this country.

Democracies are built by respecting, through personal and institutional choices, this freedom of conscience and religion, rather than by military imposition, legal dictat, or the destruction of entire societies. The United States *Bill of Rights* embodies a principle that remains a test of genuine democracy: the free exercise of religion, that clearly implies freedom of conscience and of institutional expression of belief. The

American Constitution then prohibits that the State adopt legislation to establish an official religion or that it prefer one religion over another. From this perspective, the State should not interfere with the free exercise of religious freedom, or with one's practice of religion, nor should the State require a person to act against her or his religious views. Thus the presence of religious communities in the public sphere cannot be relegated to the celebrations of rites and ceremonies, but must be able to play an active role and to express their own vision of the human person and of the policies that rule society.

Religious Liberty Must Be Respected

As the world becomes more diversified through technology of communication, migration, cultural changes, scientific progress that involves the human condition, and the emergence of new religious communities, peace and creative living together in our globalized and interconnected societies will be possible only if freedom of religion is fully respected. Indeed, this is the human right that, in the end, guarantees all other human rights. The preservation of the American experience must remain a contribution for the peaceful and truly democratic future of our world. As [French writer] Alexis de Tocqueville so wisely remarked, "Despotism may be able to do without faith but freedom cannot." Thus, we stand for religious freedom so as to free others to become fully human.

Allow me to conclude these remarks by quoting our Holy Father, a strong advocate of religious liberty: "You are called to live with that attitude full of faith that is described in the *Letter to Diognetus*: do not deny anything of the Gospel in which you believe, but live in the midst of others with sympathy, communicating by your very way of life that humanism which is rooted in Christianity, in order to build together with all people of good will a 'city' which is more human, more just and more supportive."

Periodical and Internet Sources Bibliography

The following articles have been selected to supplement the diverse views presented in this chapter.

Ethan Bronner	"At Stanford, Clinical Training for Defense of Religious Liberty," *New York Times*, January 21, 2013.
Richard Giannone	"True and False Religious Freedom," *Huffington Post*, September 13, 2012. www.huffingtonpost.com.
Laurie Goodstein	"Bishops Are Urged to Expand Priorities," *New York Times*, November 12, 2013.
William Haun	"Why Religious Liberty Became Controversial: The Left and Jean-Jacques Rousseau," The Public Discourse, June 19, 2013. www.thepublicdiscourse.com.
Kenneth Jost	"Religious Liberty and the Ignorant Majority," *Jost on Justice* (blog), November 11, 2013. http://jostonjustice.blogspot.com.
Jon O'Brien	"Let's Celebrate Real Religious Freedom," *Huffington Post*, July 3, 2012. www.huffingtonpost.com.
Thomas Peters	"What I Wish College Students Knew About Religious Liberty," Focus, October 26, 2012. www.focus.org.
Katherine Rosario	"Why Is Religious Freedom So Important for Businesses?," *The Forge* (blog), Heritage Action for America, August 12, 2013. http://heritageaction.com.
John Stonestreet	"The Crux of Religious Liberty: Practice What We Preach," BreakPoint, November 1, 2013. www.breakpoint.org.

OPPOSING
VIEWPOINTS®
SERIES

CHAPTER 2

What Does the US Constitution Say About Religious Liberty?

Chapter Preface

In the preamble to the Declaration of Independence Thomas Jefferson wrote, "We hold these truths to be self-evident, that all men are created equal, that they are endowed by their Creator with certain unalienable Rights, that among these are Life, Liberty and the pursuit of Happiness." This concept of essential and fundamental rights has been embraced as a statement of basic human rights, and it has been invoked at seminal moments in US history by leaders such as President Abraham Lincoln in the Gettysburg Address and Dr. Martin Luther King Jr. in the "I Have a Dream" speech. However, the understanding of religious liberty as a fundamental right has changed since the adoption of the US Constitution in 1787. Religious liberty was first codified in the First Amendment, which was ratified in 1791 and begins by prohibiting the establishment of a state religion and of laws that infringe on the free exercise of religion. This priority placement is no accident: the framers of the Constitution were reacting to the political and religious climate of their day.

In the mid-eighteenth century the American colonies were swept by an evangelical Christian movement known as the First Great Awakening, a cultural response to the Enlightenment, a period during the late seventeenth and early eighteenth centuries that emphasized the use of reason in scientific and philosophic inquiry. Fervent preaching characterized the First Great Awakening, inspiring churchgoers to seek a more personal relationship with their faith in a time when ritual and formal liturgy was the way most Christians worshipped. These passionate preachers—who were often Presbyterian, Baptist, or Congregationalist—were opposed by those— often Anglican or Quaker—who felt such sermons were too emotional and disruptive. Many evangelicals were itinerant preachers, meaning they had no congregation and traveled around preaching, or they were lay preachers, meaning they were unordained and had no formal training. Evangelical women sometimes preached, which was especially objectionable at this time in history, when women's roles and rights were limited. Soon many evangelicals were arrested, imprisoned, and even excommunicated. Colonies that provided state support to specific churches faced opposition from those denominations that were left out, creating a climate for which many people felt religious disestablishment was the only remedy.

In light of this background, the words of the First Amendment to the US Constitution take on greater dimension: "Congress shall make no law respecting an establishment of religion, or prohibiting the free exercise thereof; or abridging the freedom of speech, or of the press; or the right of the people peaceably to assemble, and to petition the government for a redress of grievances." The framers were not prescient; they were a product of the time in which they lived. The First Amendment was nonetheless groundbreaking—no other Western nation at that time eschewed state religion like the United States did. The Constitution was a unique approach to modern democracy, famously celebrated by nineteenth-century French writer Alexis de Tocqueville in his two-volume *Democracy in America* (1835 and 1870) as the "Great American Experiment." It is an experiment that many other nations have since tried to replicate. The authors of the following viewpoints debate what they believe the US Constitution says about religious liberty.

❚ *"The right to religious freedom is en-*
shrined in our Constitution."

The US Constitution Provides Clear Protections for Religious Liberty

Melissa Moschella

In the following viewpoint, Melissa Moschella argues that the First Amendment is being misinterpreted in the twenty-first century. She maintains that the mandate issued by the US Department of Health and Human Services (HHS) that employers must provide health care coverage for their employees that includes birth control is unconstitutional because it amounts to the federal government's interfering directly with how religious organizations operate. Moschella also contends that the Religious Freedom Restoration Act of 1993 protects against government interference with religious organizations and should apply to the HHS mandate. She concludes that the need to fight for religious liberty in the United States is immediate and serious, because this right is fundamental to humanity. Melissa Moschella is a writer for Public Discourse, *an online publication of the Witherspoon Institute, a public policy research center.*

As you read, consider the following questions:

1. What is the historical understanding of the First Amendment, according to Moschella?

2. How does the Religious Freedom Restoration Act protect religious liberty, according to the author?

3. According to Moschella, why is religious freedom a moral right and not just a legal one?

Religious freedom, which includes protection of conscience rights more generally, has been a core principle in our nation's history since even before the official founding of the United States. Many of America's first European settlers came here in search of religious freedom. Some of the world's first experiments in genuine religious toleration happened in the American colonies. And freedom of religion, together with freedom of conscience, was a central concern of America's founding fathers. Thomas Jefferson, for example, declared, "No provision in our Constitution ought to be dearer to man than that which protects the rights of conscience against the enterprises of the civil authority." George Washington himself likewise said, "The conscientious scruples of all men should be treated with great delicacy and tenderness; and it is my wish and desire, that the laws may always be extensively accommodated to them." And James Madison, a key defender of religious freedom and author of the First Amendment, said: "Conscience is the most sacred of all property."

The right to religious freedom is enshrined in our Constitution. The First Amendment reads: "Congress shall make no law respecting an establishment of religion, or prohibiting the free exercise thereof." Note that the Constitution says nothing about the separation of church and state. Indeed, at the time of the founding many states had established churches and the first half of the First Amendment—the prohibition on laws "respecting an establishment of religion"—is best understood historically as forbidding the federal government from tampering with any state laws regarding religious establishments. Today, as we've seen, that establishment clause is often read in a way that would make any public references to God or religion illegal—just think of the [court] cases trying to strike "under God" from the Pledge of Allegiance—and even make it illegal to accommodate religious organizations providing important social services, as in the Massachusetts case . . . about the government contract for the United States Conference of Catholic Bishops' services to human trafficking victims. But that's far from the original meaning of the clause.

First Amendment Protections

Nonetheless, there are good and important aspects of establishment clause jurisprudence. A recent example is the *Hosanna-Tabor* case, in which the Supreme Court reaffirmed the "ministerial exemption," which allows religious organizations to hire the ministers they want without having to worry about anti-discrimination laws. The government ought to stay out of the internal affairs of religious organizations—they shouldn't, for example, have any say in who gets to be made bishop or who is appointed pastor of the local church. That's one interpretation of the establishment clause that is good and valid, and that helps to safeguard religious freedom. The Health and Human Services mandate [that requires employers to provide health care for their employees, including paying for contraceptives] runs afoul of the establishment clause because it's telling religious organizations how to carry out their ministry, and also because the extremely narrow exemption is treating some religious organizations as more religious than others, imposing an arbitrary government definition of what counts as "religious."

The other aspect of the First Amendment's protection for religious liberty is the free exercise clause: "Congress shall make no law . . . prohibiting the free exercise [of religion]."

This means that it's unconstitutional for the government to make it illegal for you to practice your faith unless there's an extremely good reason—unless, say, your faith requires you to engage in human sacrifice or in acts of terrorism. This right also can be understood to protect freedom of conscience more broadly, even when unconnected to a specific organized religion. The HHS mandate, and many of the other affronts to religious liberty that I've mentioned, clearly run afoul of the First Amendment in this regard as well.

In addition to the First Amendment to the Constitution, there is also a federal law—called the Religious Freedom Restoration Act (RFRA), passed by a bipartisan majority and signed into law by President [Bill] Clinton [in 1993]—which provides additional legal support for religious freedom. RFRA states that the government can only burden religious exercise when there's a compelling state interest at stake, and when the policy is the least-restrictive means of achieving that interest. This law currently applies only to the federal government, although many states have enacted state-RFRAs of their own. At any rate, the law *does* apply to the HHS mandate, which is an action of the federal government, and the mandate clearly fails to meet the test. The mandate is uncontroversially a burden on religion—a $2,000-per-employee fine per year for failing to comply (i.e., Catholic Charities has 70,000 employees nation-wide, so that means a whopping $140 million in fines each year)—and even if you accept the claim that the interest at stake is compelling, the means chosen are clearly not the least burdensome available. The government could easily give all women free access to contraceptives without conscripting religious employers into doing it for them.

Religion Is Not a Lifestyle Choice

Many people mistakenly think that the basis for religious freedom is relativism. On the relativistic view, there's really no truth in matters of religion; it's just about opinions or prefer-

Two-Fold Protection

The approach to the protection of religious liberty in the United States differs significantly from the approach to the protection of religious liberty in Great Britain and Canada because of the Establishment Clause [in the First Amendment to the US Constitution]. The Establishment Clause not only prohibits the federal and state governments from establishing an official church, but also prohibits any financial assistance of any kind to religious institutions for religious purposes. In addition, the Establishment Clause also prohibits as an "entanglement" with religion, any judicial interference with religiously-based decisions of religious institutions. More fundamentally, the Establishment Clause prohibits the federal and state governments from taking *any* action that "advances or inhibits religion", such as school-sponsored prayer or bible reading in the public schools, or displays of purely religious symbols on public property. In the United States then, as a matter of constitutional structure, we provide two-fold protection to religious liberty, both by prohibiting the government from "advancing or inhibiting religion"—the Establishment Clause requires that the government maintain a course of complete official neutrality toward religion—and by specifically guaranteeing religious freedom.

Robert A. Sedler, Forum on Public Policy, December 2010.

ences or feelings. Or if there is a truth on religious matters we really can't know it. So we should let people do what they want. Religion on this view is like your favorite ice cream flavor, or, perhaps better, like your career choice; some religions suit some people better, other religions suit others better. And that's that.

But that's not the true basis for religious freedom. In fact, if religion were just a preference or a lifestyle choice, as many people think it is, that would take away the main reason for giving it special protection. Perhaps the treatment of religion as a hobby is precisely the reason why people are now having a hard time understanding why infringements on religious freedom are a big deal, or why people with religious objections have a right to exemptions.

The true basis for religious freedom, the reason why religious freedom is a moral right, and not just a legal right granted to us by the government, is that as human beings we have a grave obligation to seek the truth, and to follow the truth as we understand it. As [English theologian] John Henry Newman famously said, "conscience has rights because it has duties." "Conscience," according to Newman, "is a stern monitor," not an excuse to do what we feel like, as it is often treated today.

Conscience rights go to the core of what it is to be a human person: the capacity to act based not only on desires or instincts, but on judgments about what is good and bad, right and wrong—and the moral responsibility that is inseparable from that capacity. To force a person to act contrary to conscience is to force him to violate his moral integrity. It is an assault on the person at his core, much worse than any merely physical harm. . . . That is why heroic individuals—including the many martyrs we venerate in the Church, and even our nation's founders—have chosen to risk or suffer deprivation, imprisonment, and even death rather than compromise on matters of conscience. Such individuals are inspirations to us all. But the governments they lived under are not.

That's why America's founders were so adamant about the protection of religious liberty and conscience rights as fundamental to a free and just society. And that's why the Religious Freedom Restoration Act gets things exactly right when it forbids the government from burdening religious practice unless there really is no other way to achieve a genuinely compelling state interest.

Religious Liberty Under Fire

So where does this leave us? It is clear that there are grave, serious, and growing threats to religious freedom in our nation today. It is clear that it's no exaggeration to claim that religious freedom is under fire. To preserve our rights and the rights of every citizen, we need to make our voices heard. Ignorance and complacency are our worst enemies.

James Madison offered some words of advice to his fellow patriots after the [American] Revolution that are as relevant today as they were then:

> It is proper to take alarm at the first experiment on our liberties. We hold this prudent jealousy to be the first duty of Citizens, and one of the noblest characteristics of the late Revolution. The free men of America did not wait till usurped power had strengthened itself by exercise, and entangled the question in precedents. They saw all the consequences in the principle, and they avoided the consequences by denying the principle.

In other words, we cannot wait until our liberties are irrevocably lost before we start fighting to protect them. And when we fight for religious freedom—peacefully and respectfully, but without compromising our principles—we are both giving to Caesar what is Caesar's, *and* giving to God what is God's. Genuine love for our country requires us to be courageous and stand up in defense of our most fundamental right to freedom of religion.

| "Contrary to what many believe, there is no federal right to freedom of religion."

The US Constitution Does Not Guarantee Religious Liberty

Monte Kuligowski

In the following viewpoint, Monte Kuligowski debunks the notion that the US Constitution grants citizens freedom of religion. He argues that the Constitution only guarantees the right for states to determine their own religious practices without interference from the federal government. Kuligowski concludes that over time interpretation of the Constitution has changed drastically, and now people believe that the federal government protects the religious liberty of individuals. Monte Kuligowski is a Virginia attorney and writer.

As you read, consider the following questions:

1. According to Kuligowski, what gives states the right to regulate religion within their boundaries, including the banning of a mosque for safety reasons?

2. What amendment was used by judicial activists to alter the intent of the First Amendment, according to Kuligowski?

3. According to the author, does the US Supreme Court have the right to amend the Constitution?

A common assumption is that a national right of freedom of religion is afforded by the U.S. Constitution. Regarding the Ground Zero mosque [an Islamic center proposed to be built in New York near Ground Zero, the site of the World Trade Center felled by terrorist in September 2001], how many times have we heard that *though the imam [Muslim religious leader] has the right to build it, maybe that wouldn't be the wisest decision*? Speaking at the 2010 White House iftar dinner [iftar is the meal taken at sunset after a day of fasting during the Muslim holy month of Ramadan], [President] Barack Obama didn't comment on the wisdom, but on the supposed right:

> "But let me be clear. As a citizen, and as President, I believe that Muslims have the same right to practice their religion as everyone else in this country. And that includes the right to build a place of worship and a community center on private property in Lower Manhattan, in accordance with local laws and ordinances. This is America. And our commitment to religious freedom must be unshakeable. The principle that people of all faiths are welcome in this country and that they will not be treated differently by their government is essential to who we are. The writ of the Founders must endure."

Now enter [African American businessman and presidential hopeful] Herman Cain in 2011. Regarding another controversial mosque proposal, this one in Tennessee, Mr. Cain recently expressed his view to a news person that localities may ban mosques. Here's how the AFP [news agency] reports the story:

"Republican presidential hopeful Herman Cain on Sunday said US communities that want to ban mosques have a right to do so, as he backed opponents of a mosque being built in Tennessee.

"'Islam is both a religion and a set of laws—Sharia laws. That's the difference between any one of our traditional religions where it's just about religious purposes,' Cain told Fox News Sunday.

"Asked whether a community, like the one in Murfreesboro, Tennessee, should be able to 'ban a mosque,' Cain replied: 'Yes, they have the right to do that.'"

That's not a politically correct answer—but it's constitutionally correct.

No Federal Right to Freedom of Religion

First, the *heretical* statements and then, I'll explain: Contrary to what many believe, there is no federal right to freedom of religion. And, people do not have an automatic right to build mosques in Tennessee or any other state.

Above, Mr. Obama says that Muslims have the right to build mosques "in accordance with local laws and ordinances." But, what if a state or local law were to prohibit the building of mosques? You can bet your bottom dollar that Obama would say that a federal right of religious freedom trumps the state law.

But contrary to what Obama believes, the writ of the Founders was to prevent the federal government from exerting central control over the states in the ordinary affairs of life, including matters of religion.

The U.S. Constitution was ratified with the assurance that "Congress shall make no law respecting an establishment of religion, or prohibiting the free exercise thereof." In context, the Constitution says what the federal government cannot do; it does not provide a nationwide right of religious freedom.

The states are not prohibited by the Constitution from either establishing religion or prohibiting free exercise. In fact, during the period the individual states ratified the Constitution and the Bill of Rights most had their own official state religions. Many states endorsed the Christian religion well into the mid-20th century.

Constitutional Federalism

In 1808, President Thomas Jefferson broke from his two predecessors and decided against issuing a national proclamation for religious exercise. Jefferson did so because of our federalist system of government created by the Constitution.

Explaining his position by letter to [Reverend] Samuel Miller [who had proposed a national day of fasting and prayer], Jefferson wrote that his decision

> "results not only from the provision that no law shall be made respecting the establishment, or free exercise, of religion, but from that also which reserves to the states the powers not delegated to the US. Certainly no power to prescribe any religious exercise, or to assume authority in religious discipline, has been delegated to the general [federal] government."

Jefferson concludes his letter to Miller by noting the practice of his predecessors. But had they examined the issue of federal jurisdiction, they "would have discovered that what might be a right in a state government, was a violation of that right when assumed by another."

The individual states have retained the power under the Constitution to regulate religion, including the right to ban mosques based on safety concerns or for that matter, for any reason. Just as some Muslim countries ban or regulate the building of churches, the individual states have retained sovereignty over such matters.

Under the actual Constitution, one state may vote to ban all mosques while another may promote and fund mosques.

In areas of retained sovereignty the states are subject only to their own constitutions. The federal government is powerless to ban or to establish or to interfere with the powers of the states. That's how the country was founded. It's called constitutional federalism. It's a system which allows for diversity among the states.

First Amendment Amended

Of course, the problem is that the First Amendment itself was amended, not by the legal process of a constitutional amendment, but by unilateral decree of the U.S. Supreme Court. The Religion Clause of the First Amendment, ratified by the states to control the power of the federal government is now used against the very states it was meant to protect. And, the federal government made itself the referee regarding what the states may and may not do.

Legal commentary and court precedent was unanimous for approximately the first 150 years of our country's constitutional history on the fact that the Bill of Rights limits the power of the federal government, not the states.

Then, in the early 20th century (1925), judicial activists on the Supreme Court got clever. Since the 14th Amendment (1868) controls the power of the states—in context of ending slavery and granting rights to the former slaves—why not use it against the states in ways never imagined?

Never mind that the 14th Amendment does not mention the Bill of Rights and has nothing to do with applying them against the states. But, since the 14th speaks of "liberty" interests why not "incorporate" some of the restrictions on the federal government from the Bill of Rights into the 14th and apply them against the states?

It was dishonest to the core—but, oh so brilliant.

Because the Court did it mildly at first and incrementally, it got away with its crime against the Constitution.

In short, that's how "Congress shall make no law respecting an establishment of religion," morphed into, "Local school districts everywhere shall cease in their time-honored religious traditions and exercises."

What is taking place via the illegal doctrine of "incorporation" is pure federal tyranny.

So, did Herman Cain get it right?

Probably not if you believe the U.S. Supreme Court has power to amend the Constitution without the amendment process. And, if you believe that central control over the states via turning the Bill of Rights on its head is valid, then Herman Cain is outrageously out of touch.

But if you believe that we must set aside decades of illegal precedent and get back to the actual Constitution and the system that made America great, then, absolutely, the Hermanator nailed it.

[Author's] Note: Above, Mr. Cain bases his position on the view that Islam is not always practiced as a valid religion, not on the view that the current state of the law is an affront to the Constitution.

*"The U.S. Constitution provides for free-
dom OF religion as well as freedom
FROM religion."*

The US Constitution Guarantees Freedom from Religion

Tony Houston

*In the following viewpoint, Tony Houston explains that the
Catholic majority in Rhode Island is trying to bring religious
symbolism into the public sphere. He maintains that the establishment clause of the First Amendment protects the nonreligious
minority in Rhode Island from being subjected to the coercive religious displays—a prayer banner, a holiday tree, and a memorial cross. Houston concludes that the only legal and fair common ground is civil law. Tony Houston is an associate professor
of Spanish at Bryant University in Rhode Island. He maintains
a blog called* The Multiversalist.

As you read, consider the following questions:

1. Why is the West Cranston prayer banner in violation of
   the establishment clause, according to Houston?

Tony Houston, "Freedom from Religion Is Real Religious Freedom," *The Multiversalist*,
June 11, 2012. Copyright © 2012 by Tony Houston. All rights reserved. Reproduced by
permission.

2. How is the Woonsocket cross in violation of the establishment clause, according to the author?

3. According to Houston, what exemptions do those operating under the Christian persecution narrative demand?

The Rhode Island Catholic establishment has a persecution complex. There are a number of recurring themes in the persecution narrative that runs through the controversies surrounding the West Cranston prayer banner, the state's holiday tree and the Woonsocket memorial cross. The premise of this persecution narrative is that there is something fundamentally undemocratic about allowing a minority to overturn the will of the majority in matters of religion. The Catholic majority is a demographic and political reality in Rhode Island, but majority rule does not always equal democracy. The U.S. Constitution provides for freedom OF religion as well as freedom FROM religion.

Freedom from Religion

The Constitutional provision against the establishment of religion is not only the law of the land, it is fundamentally democratic even where there is an identifiable majority religion. Even if Catholics represented 100% of the population, identifying an area as "Catholic" would imply a commitment to preclude all others from ever settling there. The Establishment Clause [of the First Amendment] prohibits privileging any one religion over all others, thus protecting against religious coercion. The demographic reality of a Catholic majority does not entitle Catholics to impose their religious beliefs on people of other faiths or on non-believers, yet the Catholic persecution narrative equates the refusal to privilege the majority religion with an encroachment on religious freedom.

The West Cranston prayer banner was a clear violation of the Establishment Clause. Public education is compulsory. Schoolchildren are required to frequent the facility. Arguably, the banner represented a sincere effort to be inclusive. Unfortunately, this effort overlooked non-believers as a constituency and no spirit of inclusiveness was evident in the response to challenge. To ask non-believers to look away is no solution. The Establishment Clause exists to prevent coercion in all its forms. One of the most insidious forms of coercion is the public display of religious conformity. The debate over the banner illustrates this point more effectively than the banner itself. The pledge of allegiance was recited prior to the school board meetings with the words "under God" punctuated by shrill exaggeration. The aim of this exercise was clearly to intimidate. This pugnacious display of piety was a flagrant display of intolerance. Christians admire the courage of the biblical Daniel, who was thrown to the lions for defying religious coercion, but vilified a courageous teen who acted on the same principle.

The state holiday tree is fodder for the yearly revival of the "War on Christmas" narrative. The tree is on public land and is publicly maintained. People doing public business cannot avoid it. The practice of referring to a holiday tree as such is not the result of non-believers overreacting. It is a reasonable expression of respect for diverse beliefs. Jeremiah 10:3–4 identifies cutting a tree out of the forest and decking it with gold and silver as a heathen practice, but this practice is also associated with Saturnalia, a rival religious holiday. Calling it a holiday tree still overlooks non-believers for whom the tree represents no holiday. This manufactured controversy demonstrates once more the pervasiveness of the fallacy that state recognition of the majority religion assures religious freedom. Any overreaction is from the religious majority. Non-believers have assented to the polite fiction that a holiday tree is secular.

The most recent such controversy in the area is the Woonsocket cross. The cross is arguably a religious symbol on public land and would seem, therefore, to be a violation of the Es-

The Constitution Protects the Minority from the Majority

America is *not* one nation under God, but one nation under a Constitution. The Constitution was specifically amended with the Bill of Rights to uphold individual and minority rights. On constitutional matters we do not have majority rule because the majority has no right to tyrannize the minority on matters such as race, gender, or religion. The wisest policy is one of neutrality.

Al Stefanelli, OpposingViews,
August 25, 2011. www.opposingviews.com.

tablishment Clause. Supporters have asserted that the cross is not a religious symbol, but many petulantly defend this previously obscure memorial with religious devotion. Many in the secular community are hesitant to take on this issue out of respect for the Christians it commemorates and because it is reasonable to regard the cross as a historical vestige of the community's religious heritage. The casual observer may be inclined to view the cross as a historical token of disregard for religious pluralism. Some defenders of the cross have accused the complainant of cowardice for declining to be identified. Whatever view one takes in the matter, it is in the interest of all citizens to protect dissenters from reprisals. The Freedom from Religion Foundation is providing a much needed buffer that will allow for resolution of the matter. The call to root out the dissenter betrays a view of the cross as a symbol of religious conformity.

Religious Belief Does Not Trump Civil Law

The local issues mentioned above are echoed at the national level. Religious opposition to anti-bullying initiatives, marriage equality and reproductive freedom is rife with the Christian persecution narrative. This narrative demands that Christians be granted certain exemptions in public policy for the exercise of their religious conscience. Specifically, it demands that religious bullies be allowed to express their righteous indignation in the form of intimidation, that Christian institutions be exempt from recognizing same-sex marriages and that Christian medical professionals be exempt from providing family planning services.

Citizens and institutions are bound by civil law and professionals are bound by standards set by their peers. The free exercise of conscience does not extend to any act of conscience. Christian Scientists who withhold medical treatment from their children are accountable to civil authority because the state has a compelling interest in the welfare of its most vulnerable citizens. Professionals and institutions that refuse to abide by the standards set by their peers and civil law must make way for providers who can and will.

The Only Hope for Consensus

It is often said that faith and reason are independent domains. It is a natural human tendency, however, to resolve cognitive dissonance through reason, even in matters of faith. But reason and faith are mutually exclusive. Faith does not require justification and reason welcomes challenge. When faith and reason come into conflict, the believer either defers to faith or concedes to reason. An article of faith that is submitted to a test of reason ceases to be an article of faith. Faith is only what the believer accepts without question.

Reason is the common currency of civilization. It is not the exclusive domain of elite scientists. It is also the domain of philosophers who support subjective generalizations with objective observations. We all observe, predict and generalize. Scientists just control and document more meticulously to ensure objectivity. Even theologians appropriate reason to reconcile untenable articles of faith with modern sensibilities. Civil law employs the common currency of reason. Acts of conscience must be accountable to reason, not obscured by faith. Adherents within and across faiths cannot agree on ultimate truth precisely because their mutually-contradictory claims require absolute, unconditional acceptance. Civil law is our only hope for consensus.

> "Our social world has become so inter-
> twined and complicated that general
> laws, which do not take into consider-
> ation religious liberty, may still impinge
> on it."

Interpreting the First Amendment's Commentary on Religious Liberty Is Inherently Complex

John Coleman

*In the following viewpoint, John Coleman examines modern re-
ligious liberty in the United States from a Catholic perspective.
He contends that there may be a place for a generic "civil religion" in the United States and that the federal government has
the burden of proof when overriding religious liberty for other
rights. Coleman concludes that Catholic organizations have repeatedly come into conflict with civil law but that is no reason
to force a person to compromise their faith. John Coleman is an
associate pastor at St. Ignatius Catholic Church in San Francisco, California.*

John Coleman, "One Nation Under God: Can We Please Both Church and State in a Pluralistic Society?," *America*, March 12, 2012. Copyright © 2012 by America. All rights reserved. Reproduced by permission.

As you read, consider the following questions:

1. According to Coleman, in what years did anti-Catholic forces try unsuccessfully to block a Catholic from being elected US president?

2. What two Supreme Court cases demonstrate that religious liberty is privileged above all other rights, according to Coleman?

3. What examples of religious exemptions to general law does the author give?

Many people think the adage about rendering to Caesar what belongs to Caesar and to God what belongs to God pertains primarily to the separation of church and state. Yet the statement arose from a trick question posed to Jesus about religious liberty. In his time, the Romans imposed a head tax of one denarius on every man, woman and slave aged 14 to 60, and it had to be paid in the Roman coinage. Deeply religious Jews opposed using a coin that pictured the emperor Tiberius and contained the title Caesar, Divini Augusti Filius Augustus Pontifex, which means "August Son of the Divine Augustus, High Priest." For them this represented a kind of idolatry, which compromised their monotheism. So they refused to pay the tax on religious grounds.

The Herodians and Pharisees set the question to Jesus as a trap. If he sided with the religious conscientious objectors, Jesus would lose the support of the Herodians, lackeys of the Romans, and of the Roman governor who might see the response as sedition. If Jesus allowed the payment, he would be seen by nationalists and conscientious objectors as a collaborator. But Jesus sidesteps this trap with the clever retort, "Repay to Caesar what belongs to Caesar and to God what belongs to God." Jesus refrains from clarifying what belongs to each, advising the questioners to render to Caesar that on which his face appears. Jesus also insists that there are things of God that Caesar cannot touch, saying in effect: pay as much attention to God's things as to Caesar's.

Catholics and Religious Liberty

These days, few citizens assume that religious liberty is principally a gift to them derived from the good graces of the state. Rather, as the U.S. Declaration of Independence puts it, religious liberty is an inalienable right from the Creator. We honor the First Amendment principle that government not establish or define religion or impede its free exercise. The First Amendment is an act of epistemic humility, in that the state admits it has no competency to adjudicate on matters religious. If the establishment clause reminds religious groups that they have no legitimate mandate to impose their religious truths on the pluralist majority, the free-exercise clause shows that the metaphor of a so-called wall of separation cuts both ways.

U.S. Catholics have had good reason to treasure the First Amendment. They were once persecuted or held as second-class citizens in colonies that had religious establishments. Their attempt to gain religious liberty from English persecution by starting the Crown Colony of Maryland, where they extended religious liberty to others, was undercut when a new majority established there the Church of England. The papal emissaries sent to Paris [France] to confer with Benjamin Franklin [American ambassador to France at the time] about the appointment of a bishop for the United States were astounded to learn that the government did not regulate, control or try to influence the choice. Despite the denial of their religious rights by Know-Nothing, nativist, anti-immigrant and anti-Catholic forces (and the burning of Catholic churches and the killing of Catholics in Philadelphia in the 1840s) and despite the societal forces in 1928 and 1960 that tried—against Article 6 of the Constitution—to keep a Catholic from being elected president, the Constitution has protected Catholic liberty. And when Catholics fought an attempt in Oregon to forbid students from attending religious schools, the Supreme Court protected their rights (*Pierce v. Society of Sisters*) in 1925.

One could expect Catholics to be supportive of the religious liberty of other minorities—Jews, Muslims and Mormons. Recently, when a group of prominent Catholics issued a statement condemning anti-Mormon bigotry in the current presidential election [2012], one signatory was the great grandson of the former governor of New York State and Catholic presidential nominee Al Smith.

An American Jesuit scholar, John Courtney Murray, was the principal architect of the Second Vatican Council's decree "Declaration on Religious Freedom," which was subtitled "On the Right of the Person and of Communities to Social and Civil Freedom in Matters Religious." The ground for religious freedom, the document asserts, is that persons "should act on their own judgment, enjoying and making use of a responsible freedom, not driven by coercion." It notes that "all people are bound to seek the truth," but that obligation rests "upon the human conscience" and that "the truth cannot impose itself except by virtue of its own truth." The document goes on to state: "The human person has a right to religious freedom. This freedom means that all are to be immune from coercion on the part of individuals or of social groups and of any human power, in such wise that no one is to be forced to act in a manner contrary to his own beliefs, whether privately or publicly, whether alone or in association with others, within due limits."

The Right to Religious Freedom

Even for those we think in error, the right to religious freedom exists unimpeded. As the decree states, no one should "be forced to act in a manner contrary to his conscience. Nor, on the other hand, is he to be restrained from acting in accordance with his conscience. . . . The act of faith is of its very nature a free act." Not even God coerces faith. "Religious communities," the document continues, "also have the right not to be hindered in their public teaching and witness to their faith." The document cautions, however, that they should "refrain from any manner of action which might seem to carry a hint of coercion or of a kind of persuasion that would be dishonorable or unworthy." It also says, "It comes within the meaning of religious freedom that religious communities should not be prohibited from freely undertaking to show the special value of their doctrine in what concerns the organization of society and the inspiration of the whole of human activity." Finally, religious communities have the right "to establish educational, cultural, charitable and social organizations under the impulse of their own religious sense."

Not everyone would agree with this Catholic construal of religious liberty. Nor does everyone agree on a single interpretation of the establishment and free-exercise clauses in the Bill of Rights, although most Americans accept them. Is the establishment clause a function of the free-exercise clause, or does it take the indispensably primary role? Can government accommodate the religious sensibilities of a majority by a kind of "civil religion," which allows acknowledgement of "under God" in the Pledge of Allegiance and "in God we trust" on U.S. coinage? Remember that the U.S. Court of Appeals for the Ninth Circuit, in California, tried to rule the phrase "under God" in our Pledge of Allegiance unconstitutional; others have tried to stop the hiring of chaplains in the U.S. military and Congress. Some would disjoin the religion clauses from the other clauses of the First Amendment about freedom of speech and assembly and try to privatize religious liberty. They would not let religious groups show through public argument how their view has relevance to wider societal activities. These interpreters hide behind Jefferson's metaphor of a "wall of separation" and forget his injunction that "all men should be free to profess and by argument to maintain their opinions in matters of religion and the same should in no wise diminish, enlarge or affect their civic capacities."

Seeking a Balance

Recently, *The New York Times* ran a series of articles about newly perceived threats to religious liberty. A Sikh commentator noted ways by which wearing a turban has been discriminated against: Title VII of the Civil Rights Act was interpreted to mean that employers can segregate their Sikh employees from customers. Others have tried to keep Muslims from building their mosques. In the series, Michael W. McConnell, a former federal judge and First Amendment specialist, was quoted as saying, "Whatever its source, any effort to confine religious people and their ideas to an innocuous ceremonial role in public life is a threat to religious liberty and to American democracy." Anyone who has studied the history of the First Amendment knows that it involves seeking a balance that everyone can live with.

Only the naive would expect any easy consensus on interpreting the religion clauses. Is religious liberty just one freedom among others, one that can be easily traded off if there is a conflict of rights? Or was the Supreme Court correct when it claimed, in two important cases (*Sherbert v. Werner*, 1963, and *Wisconsin v. Yoder*, 1980), that religious liberty is privileged among rights and that the government must show a "compelling" public interest to override it for some other right, and must do so in a way least restrictive or burdensome to religion? These two cases feed some contemporary claims regarding new threats to religious liberty.

Catholic and other religious voices claimed religious discrimination when courts decided that the adoption and foster-child agencies of Catholic Charities must accommodate same-sex couples in Illinois (the agencies had been willing to refer such couples to other adoption groups). A judge ruled that "no group has a constitutional right to a government contract," thus dismissing any religious liberty claims. The chief counsel of the U.S. Conference of Catholic Bishops rejoined: "It is true that the church does not have a First Amendment right to a government contract, but it does have a First Amendment right not to be excluded from a contract based on its religious beliefs."

Similar complaints were raised when the Department of Health and Human Services rescinded a contract with Catholic Relief Services [C.R.S.] for the care of victims of sex trafficking. Although outside evaluators considered their work superior to that of those who won the contract, C.R.S. would not directly provide abortion services, which made the organization ineligible for the contract. Recently, many Catholic leaders protested a proposed federal mandate that church institutions provide insurance for employees that covers contraception, sterilization and access to abortifacient pills. They claim that mandates violate their religious freedom to follow their consciences on matters of abortion and contraception.

These two issues raise vexing issues of religious liberty. Will a justice of the peace whose conscience opposes same-sex marriage be forced to perform such marriages, even if other justices of the peace are available and willing to do so? Such a decision was made recently in the Netherlands. In some U.S. states, nurses and doctors who believe abortion is wrongful killing must assist with the procedure or risk losing their professional license. Vanderbilt University banned Christian groups from meeting on campus because their bylaws would disqualify an atheist from membership.

Religious Exemptions

Not every general law precludes some religious exemptions, of course; Jews and Christians were exempt from Prohibition, under the rubric of their religious liturgies. Similarly, religious pacifists are not bound to military conscription out of respect for religious liberty. On the vexing issues of abortion and same-sex marriage, society must try to accommodate the claimed rights of some with the religious exemptions of others who do not accept the morality of what is allowed by law. Overturning religious liberty rights should always demand that government show a substantial legal and social burden in order to disallow religious exemptions. Whatever one may think about the adoption of same-sex marriage in New York, care was given—as it was not in other states—to protect the religious exemptions of those who oppose the practice.

Our social world has become so intertwined and complicated that general laws, which do not take into consideration religious liberty, may still impinge on it. In 2006, when the House of Representatives passed a law making it a crime to aid or abet an illegal immigrant, the law was so far-reaching that a church offering shelter, meals or other pastoral outreach to such immigrants would be subject to severe criminal penalty. The Senate did not pass the law. Perhaps it did not because Cardinal Roger Mahony of Los Angeles publicly instructed his priests and other diocesan pastoral workers not to cooperate with it if it passed. He claimed, rightly, that it would infringe on part of any church's reason for being—caring for those in need.

Religious Civil Disobedience

Nor is it only religious people who feel the sting of new arguments about religious liberty. An army soldier is working to get atheist chaplains into the armed services, claiming that the present arrangement violates the establishment clause because it prefers religion. Proposals are circulating in the legislature of the State of Washington that envision mandated abortion coverage in the insurance provisions of all employers. We face another conflict of "claimed" rights, but the religious conscience must strenuously resist being coerced into moral evils by governmental ukases [decrees]. No one should be naive.

Religious civil disobedience may grow, if the government attempts to force religious believers to betray their consciences. An issue on the horizon involves extensions of assisted suicide laws, as they exist in Oregon. Will any nurse or doctor be forced to cooperate?

There is no magic bullet to solve complicated religious liberty cases. But some kinds of legislative efforts might require religious Americans to choose: compromise their faith, or be forced into a privatized religion that betrays the more public dictates of their faith or engage in civil disobedience. Our society needs more careful discussion and vigilance on the issue of what belongs to Caesar and what belongs to God if all of us, religious or not, are to live together and work for the common good of all.

> "Organized prayer in the public school setting, whether in the classroom or at a school-sponsored event, is unconstitutional."

Restricting Religious Expression in Schools Is Constitutional

Anti-Defamation League

In the following viewpoint, the Anti-Defamation League (ADL) contends that while it is not against the law for students to pray in school, their prayers cannot obstruct curriculum, be coercive, or be supported by the school administration in any way. It also maintains that athletic events, graduation ceremonies, and other school-sponsored student activities may not have Bible readers, prayer, or other religious content. The ADL concludes that any public school endorsement of religion is unconstitutional. Founded in 1913 to fight anti-Semitism, the Anti-Defamation League is a nonprofit organization that fights bigotry, defends democratic ideals, and protects civil rights.

As you read, consider the following questions:

1. According to the Anti-Defamation League, is voluntary, student-led prayer in a classroom unconstitutional?

2. Why did the Supreme Court determine that attendance at football games and graduation could not be considered voluntary, according to the author?

3. According to the Anti-Defamation League, is it constitutional for teachers to observe student-initiated and led prayer?

Organized prayer in the public school setting, whether in the classroom or at a school-sponsored event, is unconstitutional. The only type of prayer that is constitutionally permissible is private, voluntary student prayer that does not interfere with the school's educational mission.

May students pray? Students have the right to engage in voluntary individual prayer that is not coercive and does not substantially disrupt the school's educational mission and activities. For example, all students have the right to say a blessing before eating a meal. However, school officials must not promote or encourage a student's personal prayer. Students may engage with other students in religious activity during non-curricular periods as long as the activity is not coercive or disruptive. In addition, while students may speak about religious topics with their peers, school officials should intercede if such discussions become religious harassment. It is essential that private religious activity not materially disrupt the school's educational mission and activities. Personal religious activity may not interfere with the rights or well-being of other students, and the threat of student harassment and pressure must be carefully monitored. It is also critical to ensure that the religious activity is actually student-initiated, and that no school employee supervises or participates in the activity. Any school promotion or endorsement of a student's private religious activity is unconstitutional.

Are vocal prayer and Bible reading in the classroom permitted? Vocal denominational or nondenominational prayer, or ceremonial reading from the Bible, are unconstitutional practices in the public school classroom. It is legally irrelevant if the prayer or Bible reading is voluntary, or if students may be excused from the activity or classroom during the prayer. Student volunteers may not offer prayers for recitation. Similarly, student volunteers are prohibited from broadcasting prayers over a school intercom system into the classroom.

Can a school or state require a moment of silence in the classroom? The U.S. Supreme Court struck down a statute requiring a moment of silence which students could use for silent prayer or meditation because it was enacted for the purpose of advancing religion. Similarly, one Federal Appeals Court struck down a moment of silence statute because it had a religious purpose. More recently, however, four other Federal Courts of Appeals upheld moment or minute of silence statutes. In those cases, the courts found that statutes in question and their legislative histories did not have a religious purpose or the effect of advancing religion. Based on the Supreme Court decision and these Federal Courts of Appeals decisions, if the language or legislative history of a moment of silence law or policy has a religious purpose, advances religion, *or* is entangled with religion, it is unconstitutional. Furthermore, a moment of silence law or policy—regardless of whether its language and legislative history reflect a secular purpose and effect—will be unconstitutional if the statute is implemented in any way that encourages or discourages students to pray or engage in other religious activity.

Prayer at School Events

Can there be prayer before or after athletic events or activities? A school district's policy of permitting student-led, student-initiated prayer before football games is unconstitutional. It is also unconstitutional for a school official, including a coach, to initiate, lead, or participate in a team in prayer. Nor may a school official ask a team member or any other student to initiate or lead a prayer before, during or after a public or school-sponsored athletic activity or event. It is also unconstitutional for a member of the clergy to offer prayers before or after public school athletic activities or events. Voluntary prayer presented and led by students without official permission or sanction may be constitutional, provided that it is not coercive in any way.

Can there be prayer at graduation ceremonies? Prayers delivered by clergy at official public school graduation ceremonies are unconstitutional. The fact that a prayer is nondenominational or voluntary does not render it constitutional. The U. S. Supreme Court has not specifically ruled on whether student-initiated, graduation prayer is constitutional, and the lower Federal courts disagree on the issue. However, when the Supreme Court ruled in *Santa Fe Independent School Dist. v. Doe* that a district policy allowing student-initiated and student-led prayer before football games was unconstitutional, it effectively ruled-out the possibility that any district policy allowing student-initiated and student-led prayers would be permissible at graduation ceremonies. Moreover, in both *Santa Fe v. Doe* and *Lee v. Weisman*, the Supreme Court expressed particular concern that students could be coerced, through pressure from their peers and others, into praying during school events such as football games and graduation ceremonies. This danger exists regardless of whether it is a member of the clergy or a student who offers the prayer.

The Court also emphasized in *Weisman* and *Santa Fe* that attendance at major school events like graduation or football games should not be considered "voluntary" even if authorities officially designate it as such. Weekly football games and high school graduation are central parts of student life and students should be able to attend these events without fear of religious coercion. However, baccalaureate services, which are distinct and separate from official graduation ceremonies, may constitutionally include prayers and religious sermons. Such events must be privately sponsored and must not be led or sponsored by school personnel. Any school endorsement of such events should be actively discouraged.

Can there be prayer at school assemblies? School officials, employees or outsiders must not offer prayers at school assemblies. Even if attendance is voluntary, students may not deliver prayers at school assemblies either. Student-initiated prayer at school assemblies is unconstitutional even if the prayer is non-proselytizing and nonsectarian.

School Personnel and Prayer

May teachers pray in school? It is unconstitutional for teachers to pray with or in the presence of students in school or in their capacities as teachers or representatives of the school. Indeed, teachers may have their free speech and free exercise rights to speak about religious matters and otherwise say prayers in the presence of students abridged in an effort to ensure that there is no appearance that the school is violating the Establishment Clause. Because teachers hold such a special status in the school and are viewed as government officials speaking to a group that is both a captive audience and extremely impressionable, religious speech by teachers or other school personnel will be seen as a state endorsement of religion. The Supreme Court has said that "the interest of the State in avoiding an Establishment Clause violation 'may be [a] compelling' one justifying an abridgement of free speech otherwise protected by the First Amendment. . . ." It is also impermissible for a teacher to read the Bible in front of students during a daily silent reading period.

Can school boards say prayers prior to their meetings? The Supreme Court has upheld the right of legislative or deliberative bodies such as state legislatures to open their sessions with prayer. At least two Federal Courts of Appeals, however, have struck down prayers as unconstitutional in the school board context. Significantly, both courts found that due the close relationship of schools boards to public schools and students, such entities do not fall within the Supreme Court's meaning of legislative or deliberative body. As a result, the courts in reaching their decisions applied the established standards for prayer in the public schools to the school boards.

Sample Scenario: Football Coaches

On the day of the Central Valley High School football championship, the coach gave his team a last-minute pep talk in the Bulldogs' locker room. He then led the team in a prayer, as he traditionally did before each athletic event. Richard Nelson, a student, felt uncomfortable reciting the prayer because he was an atheist. He mentioned his discomfort to the coach who responded that Richard should simply stand in silence or feel free to leave the room while his teammates prayed together.

Is the team prayer constitutional? Is the coach's solution viable?

The team prayer led by Richard Nelson's coach is unconstitutional and the coach's offered solution is unacceptable. He has created an environment where Richard will feel isolated and as if he belonged to this group less than the other athletes. Moreover, as a school official, the coach cannot endorse religion as he is doing here.

Sample Scenario: Students

Every day at recess, Jessica Lewis, a fourth-grade student, sits under a tree in the schoolyard, recites prayers, and engages her classmates in discussions of a religious nature. The recess monitor, unsure of whether Jessica's activities violate the school's prohibition against classroom prayer, alerts school officials who forbid Jessica's recess prayers and discussions. Jessica's mother threatens to sue the school officials, claiming that their interference with her daughter's activities was unconstitutional.

Does Mrs. Lewis have a valid claim? How should the school respond?

Public Schools Cannot Teach Creationism

The First Amendment of the US Constitution contains the "Establishment Clause", which prohibits the government from promoting or advancing religion. The US Supreme Court, the highest court in the country, has been particularly vigilant about enforcing this principle in public schools because of compulsory attendance laws, the vulnerability of children, and the special trust that families place in the government to educate their children with exploiting that opportunity to religiously indoctrinate them. As a result, the Supreme Court and lower courts have repeatedly rejected both efforts to incorporate instruction in creationism, creation-science, and intelligent design into public school curricula and efforts to undermine the teaching of evolution because of its perceived conflict with the Bible. After each judicial defeat, however, creationists have adapted their tactics and unrepentantly pressed forward, prompting many to comment on the irony of an evolving anti-evolution movement.

Heather Weaver, Index on Censorship, *December 2011.*

The school should allow Jessica Lewis to engage in prayer and religious discussions with her classmates during recess provided that her activity is not disruptive and does not coerce or otherwise infringe upon the rights of other students.

Sample Scenario: Teachers

Prior to school hours on a September morning a group of students from Pines Middle School hold a student-initiated, led and run prayer event in front of the school flag pole. Student participation in the event is completely voluntary. Ms. Lake, a seventh grade social studies teacher, sees the students praying on her way to the school building. She stops, joins with the group of students, bows her head, and prays with the students. Mr. Jones, a Pines Middle School teacher also on his way into the school building, sees and hears Ms. Lake praying with the students. Mr. Jones reports Ms. Lake's conduct to Principal Franks.

Was Ms. Lake's participation in the student prayer event permissible?

No. Provided that the flag pole prayer event was truly student initiated, led, run, and voluntary, student participation in the event was permissible. Furthermore, it is permissible for a teacher or administrator to be at the event in a non-participatory manner to ensure that students comply with school rules or policies. However, Ms. Lake's participation in the event was impermissible because it constituted an unconstitutional school endorsement of religion.

Sample Scenario: School Events

A school district is reviewing its graduation ceremony policy. The policy calls on a member of the local clergy to deliver a "non-sectarian, non-proselytizing" prayer at the start of the ceremony. After the parent of a graduating senior complains, the school district would like to substitute a student who is elected by his or her peers to deliver the prayer instead.

Can the school district substitute a student for a local clergy person?

No. Neither is acceptable. Schools may not arrange to allow prayer at an event. Student prayer is limited to prayer that is personal, voluntary and non-disruptive. So long as the prayer is in any way sanctioned or controlled by the district, at an official event using the school's loudspeaker and podium, such prayer is prohibited.

> "The Supreme Court has held that student expressive activity—including prayer—cannot be impeded by the public school unless the activity creates a material and substantial disruption to the school's ability to fulfill its educational goals."

Restricting Religious Expression in Schools Is Unconstitutional

Alliance Defending Freedom

In the following viewpoint, the Alliance Defending Freedom (ADF) addresses parents, students, and educators to promote a national student-led prayer gathering at the school flagpole called See You at the Pole (SYATP). The ADF maintains that students have the right to advertise SYATP and discuss other religious matters with other students as part of their First Amendment rights to free speech and expression. The ADF further contends that if secular student groups can advertise with the sanction of school administration over the public-address system, on bulletin boards, and via handouts, then so can the students running SYATP events. The ADF concludes that schools can permit religious speech without endorsing religion. The Alliance Defending Freedom is a Christian ministry working within the legal system to advocate for religious liberty and the sanctity of life, marriage, and family.

As you read, consider the following questions:

1. According to the Alliance Defending Freedom, are teachers' rights to freedom of speech and expression enforceable when they are at school?

2. In what US Supreme Court case was it decided that student religious expression at school did not imply school support of said expression, according to the author?

3. According to the Alliance Defending Freedom, how can a school exempt itself from endorsing private religious speech delivered in a school setting?

The Alliance Defense Fund (ADF) is a legal alliance defending the right to hear and speak the Truth through strategy, training, funding, and litigation. We seek to resolve disputes through education of public officials regarding the constitutional rights of our clients. When necessary, we litigate to secure these rights. The ADF has participated in many of the recent court decisions governing students' religious and free speech rights in public schools, including *Good News Club v. Milford Central School District* (2001) (holding that the First Amendment protects student religious speech).

On Wednesday, September 28, 2011, students around the United States will participate in See You at the Pole (SYATP)—a student-organized, student-led gathering at the school flagpole where students will pray for their school, friends, teachers, government, and nation. Our government and courts have spoken: Students have a constitutional right to participate in SYATP through prayer and worship activities.

Furthermore, students have an individual constitutional right to inform their fellow students about the SYATP event as long as they do not materially disrupt the academic process while doing so. In addition, if the school allows individual students or student clubs to advertise events through school bulletin boards, school PA systems, general posting of student flyers, or other means, the school *cannot* forbid the same means of advertising the SYATP event. It is our hope that the following discussion will clarify this important area of the law and allow school districts and school officials to avoid needless litigation.

Religious Speech Is Protected

It is a fundamental principle of constitutional law that government bodies—including public schools—may not suppress or exclude the speech of private parties—including public school students—just because the speech is religious or contains a religious perspective. This principle cannot be denied without undermining the essential First Amendment guarantees of free speech and religious freedom.

It is equally true that religious speech is protected by the First Amendment and may not be singled out for discrimination. As the Supreme Court has stated:

> Our precedent establishes that private religious speech, far from being a First Amendment orphan, is as fully protected under the Free Speech Clause as secular private expression.

Importantly, the Supreme Court recently stated that public schools cannot restrict religious speech simply because it may be perceived by some as "offensive" or "controversial." . . . As the Third Circuit Court of Appeals put it in summarizing Supreme Court case law, "The Supreme Court has held time and again, both within and outside of the school context, that the mere fact that someone might take offense at the content of speech is not sufficient justification for prohibiting it."

"It can hardly be argued that either students or teachers shed their constitutional rights to freedom of speech or expression at the schoolhouse gate." The Supreme Court has squarely stated that a student's free speech rights apply "when [they are] in the cafeteria, or on the playing field, or on the campus during the authorized hours. . . ." This includes prayer: "nothing in the Constitution as interpreted by this Court prohibits any public school student from voluntarily praying at any time before, during, or after the schoolday."

Indeed, in *Daugherty v. Vanguard Charter School Academy* a federal district court rejected a legal challenge to SYATP, holding that student prayer at the school flagpole was entirely permissible.

Prayer Cannot Be Impeded

The Supreme Court has held that student expressive activity—including prayer—cannot be impeded by the public school unless the activity creates a material and substantial disruption to the school's ability to fulfill its educational goals. Any attempt to restrict such speech is unconstitutional where there has been "no finding and no showing that engaging [in the activity] would 'materially and substantially interfere with the requirements of appropriate discipline in the operation of the school.'"

Moreover, the Supreme Court has stated that the standard of "material and substantial disruption" cannot be met merely by the *possibility* of disruption. In the Court's words, "undifferentiated fear or apprehension of disturbance is not enough to overcome the right to freedom of expression."

> In our system, state-operated schools may not be enclaves of totalitarianism. School officials do not possess absolute authority over their students. Students in school as well as out of school are persons under our Constitution. They are possessed of fundamental rights which the State must respect, just as they themselves must respect their obligations to the

State. In our system, students may not be regarded as closed-circuit recipients of only that which the state chooses to communicate. They may not be confined to the expressions of those sentiments that are officially approved.

This fundamental constitutional principle is applicable both inside and outside the classroom. As the Court noted [in *Tinker v. Des Moines Independent Community School District* (1969)], when a student "is in the cafeteria, or on the playing field, or on the campus during the authorized hours, he may express his opinions[.]" The SYATP event usually occurs before the beginning of classes and is designed to avoid any sort of disruption.

Schools and school officials often mistakenly believe that allowing students to engage in religious speech at school would violate the so-called "separation of church and state"—a doctrine often cited in connection with the Establishment Clause of the First Amendment. This very argument has been reviewed and rejected by the United States Supreme Court. In [*Westside School District v. Mergens* (1990)], the Supreme Court stated as a general proposition that students' private religious expression within a public school does not present any Establishment Clause problem:

[P]etitioners urge that, because the student religious meetings are held under school aegis, and because the State's compulsory attendance laws bring the students together (and thereby provide a ready-made audience for student evangelists), an objective observer in the position of a secondary school student will perceive official school support for such religious meetings. . . . We disagree.

The Establishment Clause of the First Amendment merely "requires the state to be a neutral in its relations with . . . religious believers and non-believers; it does not require the state to be their adversary." Likewise, "[s]tate power is no more to be used so as to handicap religions, than it is to favor them."

Student Religious Expression Is Constitutional

Over the past 20 years [Charles] Haynes [director of the Religious Freedom Project at the Newseum Institute] has spearheaded efforts to come up with guidelines on religious liberty in schools that were adopted by the Department of Education and made part of the 2001 No Child Left Behind law. . . .

The consensus guidelines spell out how students can pray in school, how religious clubs that had never existed before can have equal access to school facilities and how teachers can incorporate religion into the curriculum.

Matthew Brown,
Deseret News *(Salt Lake City, UT),*
June 24, 2012.

Therefore, the Establishment Clause has no applicability to stop student speech in the SYATP context.

Schools Must Remain Neutral

The Supreme Court in *Mergens* explained that a policy of equal access for religious speech conveys a message "of neutrality rather than endorsement; if a State refused to let religious groups use facilities open to others, then it would demonstrate not neutrality but hostility toward religion."

As the Supreme Court has said, "there is a crucial difference between *government* speech endorsing religion, which the Establishment Clause forbids, and *private* speech endorsing religion, which the Free Speech and Free Exercise Clauses protect." Private student speech does not violate the Establishment Clause. Student SYATP speech is private student speech.

Student Expression Protected

Just as the SYATP event itself is protected, so also is student expression advertising the SYATP event. The *Tinker* "material disruption" standard applies to all student oral expression and literature distribution during non-instructional time, regardless of religious content. School officials may not prohibit this expression out of fear that allowing religious speech will offend some members of the community. As the Supreme Court said, "in our system, undifferentiated fear or apprehension of disturbance is not enough to overcome the right to freedom of expression." Where a student wishes to peacefully distribute free literature on school grounds during non-instructional time, there simply is nothing which "might reasonably [lead] school authorities to forecast substantial disruption of or material interference with school activities. . . ." In fact, distribution of literature is inherently less disruptive than spoken expression. As the Supreme Court stated, "[o]ne need not ponder the contents of a leaflet or pamphlet in order mechanically to take it out of someone's hand, but one must listen, comprehend, decide and act in order to respond to a solicitation."

Several courts have held that the distribution of religious literature by public school students is protected speech under the First Amendment and Fourteenth Amendment. Thus, school officials may not prohibit the peaceful dissemination of information by students about the SYATP event.

It is also well settled that the government may not discriminate against private religious speech when private secular speech is permitted in the same time, place, and manner. Again, this principle applies with equal force to religious expression engaged in by students.

Any possible misperceptions that the school is "endorsing religion" can be addressed by the school clarifying that the speech is not endorsed by the school, such as through disclaimers. Several Circuits have adopted this position in the school context:

[I]t is far better to teach students about the first amendment, about the difference between private and public action, about why we tolerate divergent views. The school's proper response is to educate the audience rather than squelch the speaker. Schools may explain that they do not endorse speech by permitting it.

Thus, if the school generally allows students or student clubs to advertise events by posting flyers on school walls or bulletin boards, having announcements read over the school's PA system, or using some other method, the school *cannot* prohibit student organizers of SYATP events from advertising in the same way.

Periodical and Internet Sources Bibliography

The following articles have been selected to supplement the diverse viewpoints presented in this chapter.

Ronald Bailey
"Freedom of Religion vs. Freedom from Religion," Reason.com, February 28, 2012.

Billy Hallowell
"Today Marks the 50th Anniversary of the Prayer Ban in Public Schools (& Here's the History)," The Blaze, June 25, 2012. www.theblaze.com.

Caitlin Yoshiko Kandil
"What Is the Future of Religious Freedom in the United States?," *Moment*, March–April, 2013.

Kristopher Nelson
"Critiquing a Lay Reading of the Constitution's 'Freedom of Religion' Clauses," The Historocrat, July 7, 2012. http://historocrat.com.

James Poulos
"Obama, Religious Liberty, and the Constitution," *Forbes*, November 12, 2012.

Monica Von Dobeneck
"Concern over Muslim Prayer in West Shore Schools Raises Questions About How Districts Respond to Students' Religious Needs," PennLive, January 10, 2012. www.pennlive.com.

Joe Wolverton II
"The Establishment Clause: No Aspect of American Constitutional Liberty Is More Misunderstood, Misapplied, and Manipulated than the First Amendment's Defense of Religious Freedom," *New American*, July 4, 2011.

OPPOSING
VIEWPOINTS®
SERIES

CHAPTER 3

Is Religious Liberty Under Threat?

Chapter Preface

The United States Commission on International Religious Freedom (USCIRF) is an independent, bipartisan governmental commission dedicated to defending freedom of religion abroad. In 2010 Knox Thames, the director of policy and research for USCIRF, stated that religious liberty is the "canary in a coal mine" for other human rights. In other words, if religious liberty is restricted or suppressed, it is a clear indication that other rights are being restricted or suppressed as well. Religious liberty, therefore, is closely watched around the world by the USCIRF and human rights groups.

According to the 2011 report *Rising Restrictions on Religion* by the Pew Research Center, 21 percent of the world's nations have high or very high restrictions on religion, which affects the 59 percent of the world's population who live in those nations. The same study shows 20 percent of countries have high or very high incidences of social hostilities involving religion, which affects 48 percent of the world's population. The study also shows that these numbers had risen since 2009, with government restrictions of religious liberties increasing in 23 out of 198 countries, including the populous nations of Egypt, France, and Syria.

North Korea, with its closed borders and totalitarian government, has long been a concern of human rights groups. Reports of conditions from this country are less regular than from other countries, but infringement of religious liberty and other human rights violations is a matter of fact there, so only the severity of the suppression may change from year to year. In its 2010 annual report, the USCIRF reported that in North Korea "anyone discovered engaging in clandestine religious activity is subject to discrimination, arrest, arbitrary detention, disappearance, torture, and public execution."

Oppressive conditions, such as those in North Korea, are not new. Throughout human history, powerful governments and religious groups have asserted their dominance by restricting the rights of individuals. For example, Christianity emerged in the shadow of the Roman Empire, in which the state religion was the polytheistic Greco-Roman religion. Jews and Christians at that time were often persecuted for their monotheistic, divergent beliefs.

Twelve to fifteen hundred years later, with Christianity ascendant in the Western world, the Roman Catholic Church tried to weed out heresy and promote religious purity (at the expense of Jews, Muslims, Protestants, and other religious minorities) through the suppression of the Inquisition. The only options available to many religious minorities during the Inquisition were to profess Catholic Christianity (even if falsely) or face torture and death, and those found to be guilty lost all of their property and wealth. In the twentieth century the Christian Armenian population of Turkey, a secular nation that is home to a Muslim majority, was nearly wiped out due to violent discrimination against them for their religious differences.

In the early twenty-first century, religious liberty has become a serious concern for many Americans. In the United States many complex religious liberty issues are being hotly debated in the courts, in legislatures, in the media, and on social networks. The authors of the following viewpoints specifically debate whether religious liberty is under threat in the United States.

> "Attacks on religious freedom escalated with the creation of Obamacare, [which] has ordered American employers to provide employee health insurance that covers 'free' contraception, sterilization and abortion-inducing drugs."

Legally Mandated Birth Control Coverage Violates Employers' Religious Liberty

Alan Sears

In the following viewpoint, Alan Sears contends that US president Barack Obama and his administration are hostile toward religious liberty, despite the fact that the president has said otherwise. Sears maintains that the Obama administration has been attacking religious freedom in many ways and concludes that Obama must start promoting a public policy that preserves America's heritage of freedom. Alan Sears is president and chief executive officer of the Alliance Defending Freedom, a legal advocacy group promoting Christian values.

Alan Sears, "Religious Freedom vs. Totalitarianism," *National Catholic Register*, March 18, 2013. Copyright © 2013 by the National Catholic Register. All rights reserved. Reproduced by permission.

As you read, consider the following questions:

1. According to Sears, what two acts were passed by the US Congress to protect First Amendment freedoms?

2. How has the Obama administration attacked religious liberty, according to the author?

3. What kinds of religious oppression have Christian university and college students faced in recent years, according to Sears?

O ver the past few decades, attempts to limit religious freedom in the public square have expanded into what is nearing a hostile exile.

This hostility led the then-sitting Congress to overwhelmingly enact the federal Religious Freedom Restoration Act [in 1993] to further protect First Amendment freedoms. And it is what has now [in 2013] led a much smaller number in Congress to introduce the Health Care Conscience Rights Act to further protect those freedoms against the Affordable Care Act's abortion-pill mandate and other mandates that threaten freedom of conscience.[1]

But the abortion-pill decree is perhaps the most serious and recent incarnation of the [Barack Obama] administration's hostility to religion.

Obama Attacks Religious Liberty

At the beginning of the year [2013], Obama issued a proclamation, declaring Jan. 16 "Religious Freedom Day," noting that "each of us has the right to practice our faith openly and as we choose."

---

1. The Affordable Care Act (aka Obamacare) mandates that employers must provide medical insurance for their employees and that this insurance must include payments for contraceptives and medications that induce abortions, which many people object to on religious grounds.

But, despite this claim, throughout his administration's first term, countless Christians, Jews and others have become prisoners of administration policy that contradicts this proclamation.

Although the president won re-election with the misleading campaign slogan "Forward," his administration has taken American liberty backward with public policy, and its limits on conscience resemble the oppressive, atheistic rule of totalitarian ages past.

The president's policies reflect a rejection of the very fabric of American society and the God-given freedoms our Founding Fathers enshrined in the Constitution—in particular, religious freedom.

The Obama administration's many attacks on religious freedom include allowing U.S. taxpayer dollars to be transferred to non-governmental agencies that perform abortions abroad; defunding successful efforts to halt sex trafficking for advocates opposing abortion; discontinuing the White House tradition of sponsoring an event on National Prayer Day; ordering the Justice Department to stop defending the federal Defense of Marriage Act; and eliminating the reference to our "Creator" when quoting the Declaration of Independence.

The attacks on religious freedom escalated with the creation of Obamacare. The administration has ordered American employers to provide employee health insurance that covers "free" contraception, sterilization and abortion-inducing drugs—or face crippling fines.

Obey the Law or Go Out of Business

Christian business owners like Bill Newland, president of Hercules Industries, whom Alliance Defending Freedom represents in a lawsuit against the president's mandate, must either choose to act contrary to their religious beliefs [follow the law] or follow the dictates of their conscience and, as a result, face steep fines that could put them out of business.

People Should Pay for Their Own Contraceptives

People on the left complain that, by opposing the contraception mandate, the Church is denying women contraceptives, but that's only true if I am denied a dinner at Red Lobster because I have to pay for it out of my pocket. People who believe that also believe, with Big Brother, that Freedom equals Slavery.

F.H. Buckley, American Spectator, *April 2012.*

In the past, our cases at Alliance Defending Freedom were all about how the role of religion in America is defined. Sadly, today, they have become more about whether religion has a role at all.

The lawsuits we have filed against Obamacare, for example, are in sharp contrast to legal cases of the past that dealt with differences of opinion on what the state may limit when it comes to religion. With Obamacare, on the other hand, the administration is now trying to expunge religious expression altogether by arguing that Christian entrepreneurs cannot exercise their religious convictions even in running their own businesses.

The same applies in the marriage arena. Not too long ago, activists seeking to redefine marriage were content with branding Christians who believe in a biblical ethic regarding sexual behavior as "bigots." Now, advocates of the homosexual legal agenda want the courts and legislatures to make all those who dare oppose their demands to pay a price—whether it be going out of business, losing their jobs or remitting a hefty fine. Recently, the New Mexico Human Rights Commission assessed a young Christian photographer, whom Alliance Defending Freedom represents, thousands of dollars for declining to use her artistic talents to celebrate a "commitment ceremony" between two women.

The Effect on Campuses

Colleges and universities have also abandoned their prestigious origins as institutions dedicated to truth, marking a dramatic shift in recent years in how they deal with religious expression on campus by unjustly denying Christian students and groups access to the same rights, funding and privileges as other non-religious individuals and groups.

And, on some campuses, this attempt to limit religion on campus has turned into a full-scale expulsion of religious conviction. Eastern Michigan University, for example, expelled one of our clients, a counseling student, out of its master's program and denied her a degree simply because she followed standard procedure and referred a potential patient wanting to improve her same-sex relationship to another counselor.

As Charles Carroll, the only Catholic signatory to the Declaration of Independence, wrote, "Without morals a republic cannot subsist any length of time; they, therefore, who are decrying the Christian religion, whose morality is so sublime and pure . . . are undermining the solid foundation of morals, the best security for the duration of free governments."

President Obama's platitudes for religious freedom are never ending. They cover up the stark reality of his rejection of our First Amendment as it was intended by our Founders.

In the president's weekly address of Sept. 15, 2012, he stated, "We stand for religious freedom. And we reject the denigration of any religion."

It is time for the Obama administration to do what it says it will do—to abandon mere rhetoric, halt the attacks and promote public policy that preserves America's heritage and restores religious freedom to its rightful place.

It is time to set people of faith free.

"*[Business] owners [cannot] plausibly argue that their rights are violated because they must pay for these health-care plans.*"

Legally Mandated Birth Control Coverage Does Not Violate Employers' Religious Liberty

Barry W. Lynn

In the following viewpoint, Barry W. Lynn explains that Catholic and fundamentalist Christian business owners are fighting the Affordable Care Act because they claim it violates their religious liberty by forcing them to pay for services for their employees that the owners oppose in conscience, such as birth control. Lynn contends that religious liberty protects a person's right to make moral decisions for himself or herself, not others, and that employers do not have the right to deny their employees access to birth control. Lynn concludes that the matter will not be settled until it goes all the way to the US Supreme Court. Barry W. Lynn is the executive director of Americans United for Separa-

tion of Church and State, a nonprofit, nonpartisan, educational organization dedicated to maintaining the constitutional separation of church and state.

As you read, consider the following questions:

1. According to Lynn, who is among those leading the fight against the Affordable Care Act?

2. What three secular corporations are engaged in a legal battle against the Affordable Care Act, according to the author?

3. What is a medical condition that birth control treats for women, according to Lynn?

Should your boss be able to determine which prescription medications you take at home? Should your boss have a say in how many children you have?

Most Americans would answer a resounding "No!" to these questions. Yet if current political and legal trends continue, more and more Americans may find that their health care hinges not on what their doctors think is best for them but what their bosses believe about religion.

This curious state of affairs stems from a deliberate attempt to redefine religious freedom in America. You read that right—religious liberty. A freedom that has historically been interpreted as an individual right of self-determination is being twisted into a means of controlling others and meddling in their most personal affairs. For the sake of true freedom, this must be stopped.

Seeking Special Privilege

The Affordable Care Act mandates that certain basic services and features must be offered in employee health-care plans. Birth control is among these. Houses of worship and similar ministries are exempt from the mandate, and religiously affiliated entities (hospitals, colleges and social service groups) have been accommodated in other ways.

This is not enough for some ultra-conservative religious leaders who oppose birth control. They are insisting that any business owner should be able to deny his or her employees access to birth control no matter what the nature of the business.

At the behest of the Catholic bishops and their fundamentalist Christian allies, far-right legal groups have filed a slew of cases insisting that secular corporations and other employers have a right according to the principle of religious freedom to deny contraceptive coverage to the men and women who work for them. Among those waging this crusade are the Becket Fund for Religious Liberty, TV evangelist Pat Robertson's American Center for Law and Justice and the Alliance Defending Freedom, an organization founded by radio and TV preachers.

Secular Corporations Are Not Exempt

Several of these cases have bubbled up to the federal appeals courts. The U.S. Court of Appeals for the 7th Circuit heard arguments in one case [in May 2013] involving two firms, K&L Contractors and Grote Industries, and the following day the appeals court for the 10th Circuit heard a challenge brought by Hobby Lobby, a chain of craft stores.

These are all secular firms. K&L is a construction company, Grote makes auto-related products, and Hobby Lobby is in the retail business, hawking items such as pink flamingo wind chimes and 3-D garden gnome stickers. In each case, their owners personally oppose some forms of birth control.

Since these firms concede that they're not religious institutions, the only question is whether the evangelical Christian and Catholic owners of the companies have the right to ig-

The Free Exercise of Religion Is a Protection, Not an Exemption

The contraception mandate is a pressure point created by broad and powerful social currents, but there are many such points (abortion and same-sex "marriage" among them)....

Partisans of religious liberty should not expect the courts to be reliable allies in this fight. The relevant judicial interpretations of the Constitution are discouraging. The clause that sounds most in sympathy is the one in the First Amendment that bans Congress from "prohibiting the free exercise" of religion. But its scope is basically limited to laws meant to harm religion; it does not relieve churches and believers of burdens imposed by laws of "general applicability."

Gerard V. Bradley,
National Review, *March 5, 2012.*

nore a federal law that they disagree with on religious grounds—in this case, a law mandating birth control coverage in health-insurance plans.

They do not. The principle of religious liberty protects your right to make moral decisions for yourself, not others. Obviously, a law that required Hobby Lobby's owners to use birth control would be a gross violation of their religious liberty. But the mandate doesn't do that. It merely requires that the 22,000 employees of Hobby Lobby be given the right, if they choose, to access birth control through a health-insurance plan.

Nor can Hobby Lobby's owners plausibly argue that their rights are violated because they must pay for these health-care plans. The fact is, if we allowed everyone to opt out of paying for everything they object to on moral grounds, society would quickly grind to a halt.

Employees' Loss of Privacy

Fundamentalist Christians might refuse to pay for a public school system that teaches evolution. Conservative Muslims might refuse to pay for public museums that may contain art that offends them. More to the point, a boss who believes in spiritual healing might refuse to provide medical coverage at all, arguing that only God, not a doctor, can make you well.

In fact, if a company can refuse to cover your insurance costs for what it considers an "immoral" practice, what's to stop it from simply refusing to hire anyone who might buy contraceptives with cash from a paycheck?

Under the First Amendment, you are shielded from being forced to pay for someone else's religion. But nothing in the Constitution protects you from paying for things you just happen to object to on moral grounds. In a country as politically splintered as ours, such a la carte taxation would make it virtually impossible to get anything done.

This issue is also important from a medical perspective. Americans use birth control for many reasons—not just to limit births. Some women need birth control pills to manage serious issues such as endometriosis. Americans value their medical privacy. No one should be forced to go to their boss begging for medication they need to treat a serious condition. Religious freedom is not a license to meddle in someone else's health issues.

The appeals court rulings in these cases are unlikely to be the last word. This issue is so important there's a good chance it will land before the Supreme Court. If it does, the court should take the opportunity to make one thing very clear: As precious as it may be, religious freedom gives you no right to make moral or medical decisions for others.

> *"The NYPD's surveillance program significantly affected the lives of its [Muslim] targets for the worse, making them frightened, paranoid . . . and more inclined to practice their religion in isolation."*

American Muslims' Religious Liberty Is Threatened by Surveillance

Conor Friedersdorf

In the following viewpoint, Conor Friedersdorf discusses the long-term effects of surveillance by the New York Police Department (NYPD) on Muslims after the terrorist attacks on the United States on September 11, 2001. He contends that the NYPD racially and ethnically profiled Muslims as a counterterrorism effort, and American Muslims have been too frightened to speak out about this infringement of their civil liberties. Friedersdorf maintains that the NYPD surveillance resulted in declined attendance and participation in mosques, anxiety about wearing traditional dress in public, fear about being misunderstood, and suspicion that community members might be informants. Fried-

ersdorf concludes that if Jews or Catholics had been treated this way, the American public would be outraged at the infringement of their civil rights. Conor Friedersdorf is a writer for The Atlantic *magazine.*

As you read, consider the following questions:

1. According to Friedersdorf, who originally broke the story on the NYPD's surveillance of Muslims?

2. How many leads were generated by the NYPD surveillance of Muslims, according to the author?

3. According to Friedersdorf, what backlash did Muslims suffer when seen by members of their community while being interrogated by the NYPD?

America's largest city, an ethnically diverse, politically liberal melting pot of more than 8 million people, routinely violates the civil liberties of its racial and ethnic minorities. New York City's "Stop and Frisk" policy, the subject of a class action lawsuit, annually ensnares hundreds of thousands of innocent New Yorkers, a majority of them black and Latino. Complaints about searches sans probable cause are constant. Listen for yourself as a 17-year-old Harlem boy is stopped, called a "f——mutt" and threatened with a broken arm. Read about the part of "Stop and Frisk" that was already declared unconstitutional in federal court. See the appalled street protesters. The visible activism and vocal dissent is as it should be.

But the sustained public backlash against "Stop and Frisk" is also a reminder that Americans know comparatively little about the Muslim Americans whose communities haven't just been disproportionately impacted by NYPD [New York Police Department] attention, but exclusively targeted in a deliberate, decade-long policy of outright ethnic profiling.

As it turns out, many were too rattled to go on the record with complaints, and have spoken out for the first time only after being sought out by a coalition of civil-liberties organizations, which has compiled testimony that shows the high cost these innocents have paid merely for being Muslim in New York.

Since September 11, 2001

First, a bit of background:

The Associated Press [AP] brought the NYPD's clandestine spying on Muslims to the public's attention in a series of vital stories [beginning in 2011]. Starting shortly after the September 11 terrorist attacks, officers infiltrated Muslim communities and spied on hundreds or perhaps thousands of totally innocent Americans at mosques, colleges, and elsewhere. These officers "put American citizens under surveillance and scrutinized where they ate, prayed and worked, not because of charges of wrongdoing but because of their ethnicity," the news agency reported, citing NYPD documents. Informants were paid to bait Muslims into making inflammatory statements. The NYPD even conducted surveillance on Muslim Americans outside its jurisdiction, drawing a rebuke from an FBI field office, where a top official charged that "the department's surveillance of Muslims in the state has hindered investigations and created 'additional risks' in counterterrorism."

NYPD brass and Mayor Michael Bloomberg defend these policies as counterterrorism efforts that are necessary to keep New Yorkers safe. As you ponder the specific costs of these policies, as evocatively described below, keep in mind one thing about the ostensible benefits: "In more than six years of spying on Muslim neighborhoods, eavesdropping on conversations and cataloguing mosques," the Associated Press reported, "the New York Police Department's secret Demographics Unit never generated a lead or triggered a terrorism investigation." They acknowledged, in court testimony, having generated *zero* leads.

NYPD Surveillance Damaged Trust

Okay, now the costs. . . .

The abstract objections to police officers spying on innocent Americans based on their religion are presumably familiar to readers, so let's focus on concrete costs to the innocent victims:

- The week that AP published its investigation, "the students wouldn't come to the prayer room," the leader of a Muslim student group at a New York college said. "They felt they couldn't meet in their own space. The idea of being surveilled—for a 19- or 20-year-old—is a terrifying thing."

- A young man "who befriended a fellow mosque-goer only to find out that his friend was an NYPD undercover [informer] responded by severing his relationship with the mosque for a year. He has since returned . . . but refuses to involve himself in the mosque's activities, or to befriend anyone. He just goes to pray, and then promptly leaves, believing that anything more might put him at risk."

- Multiple imams [Muslim clerics] reported that they "avoided providing one-on-one consultations because they could never be sure that a question posed by a congregant is a sincere one, or whether it is an attempt by an informant to elicit opinions that he or she will then pass on to their handlers." Said one, "The relationship of trust and confidentiality between an imam and his congregation is no less sacred than that of pastors, rabbis or others. . . . The actions of the NYPD have compromised this sacred relationship. . . . It not only weakens the capacity of some Muslim religious leaders to serve as advisers in sensitive matters, but it also compromises their effectiveness as partners in the struggle against extremism. After all, how can a leader give guidance in matters that he or she is hesitant to discuss in any way, for fear of covert monitoring or entrapment? . . ."

Looking for Spies

- "Interviewees noted that appearing Muslim, or appearing to be a certain type of Muslim, invites unwanted attention or surveillance from law enforcement." Said one, "There's always been a sense of stereotyping about dress. But now the veil thing has become more than just about being different. It has become charged with suspicion."

- Parents are anxious about the effect on their children, and nag them accordingly. A college student said "his parents did not want him to go to Muslim Student Association events or wear his Muslim hat." Another student "who wears the niqab, or face veil," noted that "her mother asked her to stop wearing all black because she worried her dress would draw police scrutiny."

- Many regular mosque-goers have decreased their attendance, "and those who attend do so to just pray and leave, looking over their shoulders for eavesdropping spies the entire time. One young woman who is responsible for organizing youth activities in her mosque noted how congregants have internalized the need to self-edit religious Sunday school curriculum: 'It's very difficult, it's very hard, you don't know what to say, I have to think twice about the sentences I say just in case someone can come up with a different meaning to what I'm saying.'"

- "Interviewees stress that the ever-present surveillance chills—or completely silences—their speech whether they are engaging in political debate, commenting on current events, encouraging community mobilization or joking around with friends. Political organizing, civic engagement and activism are among the first casualties."

Fear of Reprisal

- Said a community organizer, "We're Arabs, we talk about politics all the time. . . . Politics is all we do! Every coffee shop, it's either [Arabic news agency] Al Jazeera or a soccer game on TV. This new idea that we must be suspicious of those who speak about politics—something's wrong." . . . "Business owners, mosque leaders and community members alike actively censor conversations, event programming, and internet usage in hopes that avoiding certain political content will keep them and their respective religious and social spaces off the NYPD's radar." And one business owner stated, "I don't allow Al Jazeera on in our hookah bar. Particularly when things flare up in the Middle East. We can't control what people start saying in response to the news, and we never know who else is in the bar listening."

- A Sunday school teacher explained that she is afraid to criticize the very policies that target her community: "I don't talk about the NYPD on Facebook. We'll put articles up, but we will never comment on them, put our own words. [The] maximum we'll say is 'it's sad that this is happening.' But we will never show our anger, that we're really, really angry. Some people aren't afraid, but I am."

- Said one young man, "I come from a family of activists. My parents, when I first told them the Associated Press story is about to break, my dad told me don't do anything about it. That was the first time my dad ever told me anything like that. This was the first time in my own family where safety trumped what was the right thing to do."

Fears of Being Misunderstood

• A community organizer states that "almost every rally and public forum I've attended in the last year begins with some type of disclaimer or callout of informants and undercovers who might be in attendance and recording the conversation. Most speakers don't even know if such a disclaimer protects them in any way, but I feel it to be a necessary announcement so that the audience participants are conscious of the environment in which we are organizing."

• "Those we interviewed also expressed concern with how terms and expressions they use in their native languages might be literally translated and misinterpreted by law enforcement. A prominent Queens business owner explained how a common Arabic phrase to denote excitement could be mistranslated into English to convey that the one is so excited that he will 'explode.' The business owner explained that such phrases, commonly used to denote emotion, are seldom used anymore."

NYPD Surveillance Breeds Suspicion

• The presence of informants who are Muslim or posing as Muslim has made everyone in these communities paranoid and mistrustful of one another, one interviewee explained: "Every other store on this street could be an informant. You start wondering about each one: how did this person get his liquor license so quickly? Or how come the cops aren't saying anything about this guy who is well known to be selling alcohol under the table, or to minors." . . .

- "Ironically, those who have been approached by the NYPD become objects of suspicion among their own peers. Interviewees who had been contacted for questioning by the FBI or by the NYPD were worried that others in their community might find out, resulting in their being viewed by their peers and neighbors with either fear or mistrust. One young man whom NYPD detectives visited at home, questioning him in front of his neighbors, describes his subsequent social marginalization: 'Nobody will trust you with things that they did trust you with before. . . . Trust is gone. My own neighbor—he doesn't say it, obviously no one says it. But I feel like it's on their faces. They know something's not right because they were there when the NYPD visited us. I assume he figured out it was just a fishing expedition, but I generally feel that they don't want to deal with us.'"

Accused of Being an Informant

For some reason, I found this passage among the most affecting:

> Nearly all interviewees thought they knew someone who was an informant or an undercover officer. The reasons provided were diverse and contradictory, reflecting the widespread internal suspicion that surveillance has triggered within the American Muslim community. Someone viewed as overly religious was suspect, while another who frequented the mosque without seeming particularly religious was equally suspect. . . . Two interviewees recalled incidents where they falsely accused someone of being an informant, leading to potentially devastating reputational consequences for the accused. One of the students who was on a Whitewater rafting trip that was attended by an undercover officer

thought he could tell who that undercover was through a process of elimination. When invited to do so during a press interview on national television, he ventured a guess. He was wrong. In his interview, he still expressed remorse: 'I have to give him a call and apologize.'

A second interviewee recalled with regret how he was suspicious about a new member of the mosque whom he noticed suddenly became very involved and active in his mosque's administration. He discussed his concerns with others at the mosque. Later on, he found out that the same man had recently lost his job and had time on his hands. He described his feelings of guilt when he noticed that his warnings had led others to be wary of this man.

NYPD Surveillance Is Unethical

There's lots more in the report. I skipped whole categories of harm in my already-too-lengthy excerpting. Suffice it to say that the NYPD's surveillance program significantly affected the lives of its targets for the worse, making them frightened, paranoid, mistrustful of one another, less willing to participate in the civic process, and more inclined to practice their religion in isolation. If Catholics or Jews were targeted by a municipal police department in this way, utterly changing the dynamic of their faith communities for years on end, Americans would be outraged, doubly so if the surveillance produced zero leads and no evidence of averting any serious crime.

Yet somehow Bloomberg presides over all this, defending it after the fact, *and* remains a darling of the center-left, constantly getting adulatory treatment from the establishment press. "First, as somebody who has lived in New York for almost thirty-five years, I have to say your stand on the non-mosque that's not at Ground Zero marked the first time I've ever written a mayor to say thanks for doing the right thing," wrote Kevin Baker, interviewing Bloomberg when *GQ* [maga-

NYPD Surveillance Violates First Amendment Rights

The First Amendment of the United States Constitution prohibits the government from impeding the free exercise of religion, abridging the freedom of speech and interfering with the right to assemble. Our research has shown that the NYPD's surveillance directly impacts First Amendment rights: American Muslims are fearful of discussing politics and current events, deterred from going to their mosques, and chilled from associating with political, civic and spiritual groups for fear of increased law enforcement attention and surveillance. The First Amendment exists to protect precisely these forms of belief and expression. Even though the NYPD does not directly prohibit American Muslims from practicing their religion or expressing political and civic opinions, NYPD policies, which characterize such expression as suspect, ultimately stifle and deter expression. Such a "chilling effect" can be a violation of the First Amendment.

Muslim American Civil Liberties Coalition,
Creating Law Enforcement Accountability & Responsibility,
and Asian American Legal Defense and Education Fund,
Mapping Muslims: NYPD Spying and Its
Impact on American Muslims, *March 11, 2013.*

zine] declared him a Man of the Year in 2010. And he was right to praise him for that stand. "Your speech did a great job of tracing the fights for immigrants' rights, the fights for religious freedom in New York, all the way back to the Flushing Remonstrance of the seventeenth century," Baker continued. "Is New York City the place, more than any other, where we have fought it out over who gets to be a full American and what that means?"

NYPD Infringes on Civil Rights

It's self-congratulation I wish NYC deserved, but it doesn't in this case. Said Bloomberg in reply, "New Yorkers, I don't know that they like each other or socialize together, but they go down the same steps to the subway, they hail a cab at the same corner, they buy their coffee at the same Starbucks, their newspaper at the same kiosk—and so people who look different, act different, sound different, smell different, dress different, whatever, they are not threatening, because you are next to them all the time." . . .

What does it say about American liberalism today that two of the most significant municipal programs abrogating the civil liberties of racial and ethnic minorities thrive in a deep blue city that also happens to be the media capital of the country . . . and the guy presiding over it remains popular? Just now he's predicting drone surveillance in New York City's future. For what it's worth, NYC Muslims, Bloomberg has never even entertained any principled objections to the Civil Rights Act of 1964.

> "Never before in our U.S. history has
> the federal government forced citizens
> to directly purchase what violates our
> beliefs."

Legalizing Abortion Endangers Religious Liberty

Mark Pattison

In the following viewpoint, Mark Pattison reports on the 2012 March for Life and National Prayer Vigil for Life in Washington, DC. The vigil was led by Daniel Cardinal DiNardo, Roman Catholic archbishop of the Galveston-Houston archdiocese in Texas, who implored young people everywhere to protect all life, whether born or unborn, and urged people to continue to fight for religious liberty. Pattison contends that DiNardo believes that pro-lifers are gaining ground as more state laws are passed to restrict abortion and likens the fight against abortion to that of the biblical David against the giant Goliath. Mark Pattison is a reporter for Catholic News Service, a media service specializing in religious news.

As you read, consider the following questions:

1. According to Pattison, how many years had the Catholic Church been fighting to end abortion in the United States when the US Department of Health and Human Services announced their mandate that all employers with health plan benefits must cover contraceptives and sterilizations?

2. According to the author, who have state attorneys begun to prosecute?

3. What new element was introduced in the 2012 procession for the National Prayer Vigil for Life, according to Pattison?

Participants at the annual March for Life were urged in advance of the march not to let themselves be compromised in their beliefs as the federal government pursues regulations that Catholic leaders say constitute an attack on conscience and religious liberty.

"I beg and pray for the young people present and all youth and young adults not to be compromised in your dedication to the protection of life of each human person, born and unborn," said Cardinal Daniel N. DiNardo of Galveston-Houston. "Keep it before your eyes and in your hearts immediately. Threats against life and against the consciences of those who say 'yes' to life must be met with timely and unwavering action, in our families and institutions, and yes, in the public square."

Cardinal DiNardo, chairman of the U.S. bishops' Committee on Pro-Life Activities, made his remarks during his homily at the Jan. 22 [2012] opening Mass for the National Prayer Vigil for Life. The overnight vigil, which included a closing Mass Jan. 23 and hourly Holy Hours in between, was conducted at the Basilica of the National Shrine of the Immaculate Conception in Washington.

The cardinal linked the 39-year struggle to end abortion on demand with Jan. 20's announcement from U.S. Health and Human Services Secretary Kathleen Sebelius that most religious organizations would have to cover contraceptives and sterilization free of charge in their employee health plans, rejecting appeals from Catholic groups to widen the exemption.

"Never before in our U.S. history has the federal government forced citizens to directly purchase what violates our beliefs," Cardinal DiNardo said, adding that the issue is "the survival of a cornerstone constitutionally protected freedom that ensures respect for conscience and religious liberty."

Cardinal DiNardo said Pope Benedict XVI addressed the issue when meeting with U.S. bishops from the Mid-Atlantic.

"Many of you have pointed out that concerted efforts have been made to deny the right of conscientious objection on the part of Catholic individuals and institutions with regard to cooperation in intrinsically evil practices. Others have spoken to me of a worrying tendency to reduce religious freedom to mere freedom of worship without guarantees of respect for freedom of conscience," he quoted Pope Benedict as saying.

"In light of last Friday's announcement about health care mandates, it seems that the Holy Father has nailed the issue in advance," Cardinal DiNardo said. "His calls for courage to counter a reductive secularism which would delegitimize the church's participation in public life and debate have targeted the issues we face in our pro-life efforts, to defend those who defend human life and to defend their religious liberty."

Gains Made in Restricting Abortions

Cardinal DiNardo pointed to gains made by pro-lifers, including "a record number of state laws that now restrict abortions. State prosecutors have begun to prosecute late-term abortionists who deny life and injure and maim women."

FOOTPRINTS IN THE SAND

© Eric Allie, Cagle Cartoons.

Cardinal-designate Timothy M. Dolan of New York, who celebrated the closing Mass, repeatedly lauded the "radiant inspiration" generated by the marchers who gather at the shrine each year.

He said that after nearly 40 years of legalized abortion, "we might be tempted to give up."

But "not us," said Cardinal-designate Dolan, president of the U.S. bishops. "Not for thousands who have stayed up all night here in prayer. Not for hundreds of thousands who will march today with the word we have received ringing in their ears."

Vigil Grows Bigger Every Year

For vigilers who spend the night in the shrine, Cardinal Dolan brought two bits of "good news" to them: "The New York Giants did win last night to go to the Super Bowl," and weather around Washington prompted a delay in the regular opening time for the federal government. "That leaves less chance to pass a new anti-life regulatory rule," he said.

Recalling the story of King David, whose anointing as king of Israel was part of the Old Testament reading for the Mass, Cardinal-designate Dolan noted that little David killed Goliath. "The New York Giants may have won, but Goliath the giant did not," he said.

The two-hour, 37-minute opening Mass featured a 39-minute entrance procession with four cardinals, 31 other bishops, 300 priests, 75 deacons and 700 priesthood and diaconate candidates and altar servers—among them what might have been the first woman in liturgical attire to take part in such a procession for the National Prayer Vigil for Life. Cardinal DiNardo said near the end of the Mass that he had invited altar servers from the Archdiocese of Galveston-Houston to come to Washington to take part.

By contrast, the closing Mass Jan. 23 was a much shorter affair, lasting only 70 minutes with a seven-minute entrance procession. Cardinal-designate Dolan was joined by three other bishops, 63 priests, five deacons and 10 servers.

Seventeen television monitors were set up around the shrine so worshippers could see the Masses from any vantage point. The number was up from 14 last year. "It seems that this just keeps getting bigger and bigger," said shrine spokeswoman Jacquelyn Hayes.

Periodical and Internet Sources Bibliography

The following articles have been selected to supplement the diverse views presented in this chapter.

Clifford R. Ennico	"Do Atheists Have a Right to a 'Religion-Free' Workplace?," Creators.com, 2010.
Imani Gandy	"Corporations Claiming 'Religious Liberty' Try to Infringe on Their Employees' Religious Liberty," RH Reality Check, October 22, 2013. http://rhrealitycheck.org.
Liberty Institute	*Undeniable: The Survey of Hostility to Religion in America*, 2013. www.libertyinstitute.org.
Ross Murray	"Does Religious Liberty Mean Bullying Your Own Flock of Believers?," *Huffington Post*, October 12, 2012. www.huffingtonpost.com.
Sarah Posner	"Why Abortion Is a Religious Liberty Issue," *Moment*, March–April, 2013.
Peter Roff	"Obamacare Birth Control Mandate Tramples Religious Liberty," *U.S. News & World Report*, February 9, 2012.
William A. Schreiner Jr.	"Not to Preach, but Religion in the Workplace Continues to Cause Disputes," *Suits by Suits* (blog), January 13, 2013. www.suitsbysuits.com.
Diala Shamas	"Muslim Spying Has Real Victims," *New York Daily News*, April 1, 2013.
Gregory C. Sisk and Michael Heise	"Muslims and Religious Liberty in the Era of 9/11: Empirical Evidence from the Federal Courts," *Iowa Law Review*, vol. 98, 2012.

OPPOSING
VIEWPOINTS®
SERIES

CHAPTER 4

What Is the Impact of Politics on Religious Liberty?

Chapter Preface

In June 2009 US president Barack Obama gave a speech to a mostly Muslim audience at Cairo University in Egypt. Never once uttering the word "terrorism," Obama made it clear that religious toleration is a part of Islam and tolerance is critical to religious liberty. He stated unequivocally, "People in every country should be free to choose and live their faith based upon the persuasion of the mind and the heart and the soul."

Around 2010, the Obama administration began a linguistic shift away from the phrase *religious freedom* and began using *freedom to worship* instead. Some people interpreted this shift as a way for the administration to placate foreign rulers who were wary of pressure from the United States to promote religious liberty where it is not welcome. Religious conservatives in the United States objected to the change in terminology, because they perceived it as an attempt to contract their religious freedoms.

"Freedom of worship" is generally regarded as a narrower concept than "religious freedom," because it refers to *how* people practice their religion, instead of *what* religion they practice. American religious conservatives argue that "freedom to worship" relegates religion to personal practice and places of worship and removes religion from the public spheres of work and school. This private-public split satisfies atheists and many liberals, who prefer that religion be kept private, but some faiths, like evangelical sects of Christianity, value public declarations of belief, including prayer and religious symbols. Consigning religious practice to the private realm thus seems to many like a constriction of rights.

As President Obama's choice of words regarding religion illustrates, politics can greatly impact religious liberty. The authors of the following viewpoints debate what this impact is and whether politics damages or protects religious liberty.

> "Faith-driven progressives insisted that society and governments uphold the fundamental notion that all people are equal in God's eyes and deserve basic dignity, freedom, political rights, and economic opportunities."

Liberal and Progressive Politics Protect Religious Liberty and Democracy

Marta Cook and John Halpin

In the following viewpoint, Marta Cook and John Halpin present the history of religious activism in the United States as evidence that progressive politicians, theologians, and other reformers during the nineteenth and early twentieth centuries advocated for Christian teachings to be directly applied to problems, such as abject poverty, that affected society in the industrial period. Cook and Halpin conclude that progressive policy making worked to protect religious liberty and freedom for all. Marta Cook is a fellows assistant and John Halpin a senior fellow at the Center for American Progress, an independent, nonpartisan, educational institute.

Marta Cook and John Halpin, "Introduction," *The Role of Faith in the Progressive Movement*, October 2010, pp. 1–3. Copyright © 2010 by Center for American Progress. All rights reserved. Reproduced by permission.

As you read, consider the following questions:

1. According to Cook and Halpin, which prominent individuals in the nineteenth century said that Christian teachings should be applied to society's problems?

2. What 1907 book encapsulates religious progressivism, according to the authors?

3. How did Pope Leo XIII encourage a generation of American Catholics, according to Cook and Halpin?

There have historically been two primary strands of progressive thought concerning the proper relationship between faith and politics—one secular and the other emerging directly from religious social values.

Secular progressive thought, associated with Enlightenment liberalism, is skeptical about particular religious claims in a pluralistic society, and insistent upon keeping religion out of politics and politics out of religion. Prominent American liberals such as Thomas Jefferson and James Madison, among others, strongly advocated freedom of conscience, religious tolerance, and strict separation of church and state as represented in the First Amendment to the U.S. Constitution. This classical liberalism placed a premium on rationality, self-determination, and personal morality above faith, church authority, and public morality. It looked to establish a constitutional order in America that would prevent the merging of religion and government that was prevalent in Europe.

Many religious authorities during this time, most notably the Catholic Church, viewed liberalism as a "sin" and worked hard to stop its spread in Europe and America before reconciling Catholic teaching with liberal democracy. They disagreed with the liberal conception of faith and politics, which was best represented by the religious freedom and disestablishment clauses of the First Amendment. But these progressive beliefs eventually triumphed in this country as most

Americans came to accept that one could freely practice their faith while keeping specific religious beliefs from taking over government and threatening the religious freedom of others.

Religious Activism Left a Mark

An equally powerful strand of progressive thought emerged directly from religious values during the social gospel movement. These reformers argued that Christians should apply their teachings to public problems. American Protestant ministers and theologians during the 19th century such as Walter Rauschenbusch espoused this belief, as did politicians such as William Jennings Bryan, and settlement founders such as Jane Addams and Ellen Gates Starr. Catholic social justice leaders such as Fr. John Ryan and Dorothy Day pushed for similar values and religious activism, and later civil rights leaders such as Dr. Martin Luther King, Jr. followed suit. Many of the most prominent social movements in American progressive history would not have been possible without the inspirational values and moral authority of socially conscious Christianity and Judaism. . . .

Progressives working within these faith traditions applied religious morality to the task of transforming American society during the industrial age away from the exploitation of workers and toward more cooperative forms of economic life. These faith-driven progressives insisted that society and governments uphold the fundamental notion that all people are equal in God's eyes and deserve basic dignity, freedom, political rights, and economic opportunities in life. Religious progressives promoted the notion of community and solidarity above concepts of individualism and materialism, and worked to stop unnecessary wars and military aggression across the globe.

Relieving Poverty

The social gospel movement and Catholic social teaching played influential roles in the progressive search for economic

Liberalism Promotes Religious Liberty

Liberalism understood from the outset that it could not abide any religious tradition that sought to influence the order of society based upon its conception of "the Good." "Private" belief could be tolerated: such belief would extend only to the immediate adherents of that faith; its adherents had to personally choose their allegiance to that faith; and any faith commitment would be the result of voluntarist choice and thus, a chosen self-limitation on the part of the faithful.

*Patrick J. Deneen, Front Porch Republic,
February 16, 2012. www.frontporchrepublic.com.*

fairness and justice in the 20th century. Both traditions promoted the belief that any true commitment to the Gospels and the example of Jesus Christ demanded followers to take concrete steps to address oppression and hardship in this world and to replace the laissez-faire attitudes of the late 19th century with a more communitarian outlook. In his famous book, *Progress and Poverty*, Henry George, a popular economist and social gospel adherent, rejected the traditional notion of religion that allowed the "rich Christian to bend on Sundays in a nicely upholstered pew . . . without any feeling of responsibility for the squalid misery that is festering but a square away."

Walter Rauschenbusch's 1907 classic book, *Christianity and the Social Crisis*, served as the most complete statement of faith-based progressivism and offered a compelling argument for the social application of the Gospels. Rauschenbusch stressed how "the essential purpose of Christianity was to transform human society into the kingdom of God by regenerating all human relations and reconstituting them in accordance with the will of God." The purpose of this argument was to show people how Christian teachings and the prophetic tradition of the Hebrew Bible could be put to use to foment social change during a period of want and suffering: "If anyone holds that religion is essentially ritual and sacramental; or that it is purely personal; or that God is on the side of the rich; or that social interest is likely to lead preachers astray; he must prove his case with his eye on the Hebrew prophets, and the burden of proof is with him."

Helping Those Less Fortunate

Rauschenbusch took on what he called "the present crisis" wrought by the industrial revolution and the rise of modern capitalism, arguing that Christian civilization could no longer withstand the injustices of contemporary times—inequality, poverty, physical deprivation and hunger, worker abuses. He believed that desperate times required genuine moral leadership, and he sought to humanize capitalism by encouraging more direct action. He supported movements such as the settlement houses—urban community centers where low-income people could go for services and classes—as well as labor organizing and solidarity, and Christian volunteerism from preachers and groups like the YMCA and the Salvation Army. Above all, Rauschenbusch counseled people to put their theological principles to work personally by adding "spiritual power along the existing and natural relations of men to direct them to truer ends and govern them by higher motives."

On the Catholic side, Pope Leo XIII's 1891 encyclical, *Rerum Novarum*, served as the intellectual and theological basis for a new generation of social activism among American Catholics. The Pope's statement on capital and labor sought to find a humane path for capitalism that respected workers and avoided the extremes of both socialism and laissez-faire conservatism. *Rerum Novarum* affirmed the state's right to intervene on behalf of citizens, endorsed unionization, and also affirmed property rights. Its teachings provided a moral and theological basis for generations of Catholic social justice reform most famously seen in Monsignor John Ryan's "Bishop's Program of Social Reconstruction" in 1919 and later actions during the New Deal.

> "The hearty and unambiguous affirmation of religious liberty leads to the secular destruction of religion and the imposition of secularism as the default worldview."

Religious Liberty Damages Religion

Benjamin Wiker

In the following viewpoint, Benjamin Wiker reasons that the fight for religious liberty for all is creating a secular state and therefore promoting nonbelief. He maintains that the oppression of faith ultimately robs individuals of their religious belief and therefore their religious liberty. Wiker contends that everything that is wrong with how religious liberty is handled in modern government began with Benedict Spinoza, a seventeenth-century radical thinker, because Spinoza promoted the natural right of every person to decide for himself what he wants to believe. Wiker concludes that Spinoza's ideas should be abandoned, and religious organizations should be left alone to govern themselves. Benjamin Wiker is a visiting associate professor of theology at Franciscan University of Steubenville in Ohio.

Benjamin Wiker, "The Puzzle of Religious Liberty," *The Catholic World Report*, January 15, 2013. www.catholicworldreport.com.

As you read, consider the following questions:

1. According to Wiker, why does religious diversity promote a secular state?

2. Why did James Madison argue that the United States needed more religious factions, according to the author?

3. According to Wiker, who invented the separation of church and state, and when did this happen?

The embrace of religious liberty as a right was memorably expressed by James Madison in his [paper] "Memorial and Remonstrance [Against Religious Assessments]" (1785). Madison, one of the great Founders, is considered to be the father of the Bill of Rights, so it would seem we'd want his opinion about the First Amendment. "The Religion . . . of every man," Madison proclaimed, "must be left to the conviction and conscience of every man; and it is the right of every man to exercise it as these may dictate. This right is in its nature an unalienable right."

In fact, Madison declared that this right was rooted in a duty, "the duty of every man to render to the Creator such homage and such only as he [i.e., every man] believes acceptable to him [presumably, but not unambiguously, God]."

A Secular State Belies Religious Liberty

Here comes the puzzler, which I'll set out in semi-syllogistic enumerated steps.

1. Today we passionately hold that we each have a right to believe, to worship, as we see fit—each of us individually. But that means everyone else has that same right.

2. The claim and practice of that right creates a diversity of beliefs, as many as there are different convictions about what homage is acceptable to the divine.

3. In order for each individual to protect himself from some other believer using government power to dictate his beliefs, he must not allow his own or anyone else's belief, anyone else's faith, to define or inform the state as the established state religion (so that the Free Exercise Clause is inextricably linked to the Establishment Clause).

4. But the result is a state defined by *no one's beliefs*, a state defined by the subtraction of all religious beliefs, that is to say, a state defined by the establishment of *unbelief*, a secular state.

But, it is precisely this state, as secular, that ever more forcefully infringes on religious liberty by actively imposing a secular worldview upon the citizenry as the default, established worldview. This view is gotten by the *subtraction* of all beliefs, including the subtraction of the particular *moral* beliefs in Christianity that stem from its doctrinal beliefs, but not merely that. It also entails the *addition* of its own moral beliefs. The HHS [US Department of Health and Human Services] mandate [that requires employers to provide health care for their employees that includes contraceptives] is just that: an attempt at forced subtraction of Christian moral beliefs, and the imposition of secular sexual beliefs in their place.

Religious Diversity Promotes Secularism

And so, the puzzler. Like Chinese handcuffs, the harder we pull on Religious Liberty to extract ourselves from the increasingly more insistent impositions of the secular state, the more we encourage religious diversity. The more religious diversity, the greater the need for a secular state which protects us from having someone else's religious beliefs imposed upon us. The more we empower a secular state defined by the subtraction of all particular religious beliefs, the more powerfully does the secular state establish *its own* secular worldview by federal force, including secular morality. Hence, the HHS trying to mandate that the Catholic Church provide coverage for contraception, abortifacients, and sterilization.

To put the puzzler in a nutshell, the hearty and unambiguous affirmation of religious liberty leads to the secular destruction of religion and the imposition of secularism as the default worldview.

This destruction is even more complete than we've implied, a point that can be made clear with our example of the Catholic Church. If it is an "unalienable right" for every man to define his religion according to his "conviction and conscience," then the Catholic Church above all violates Religious Liberty by imposing very specific theological and moral doctrines on its flock.

And so if we truly want the secular state to protect this "unalienable right" of each individual to define his religion according to his personal conviction and conscience, then the state can rightly be called in to protect the rights of individual Catholics from violations by the Catholic Church—including the Church's intransigence in not providing contraception, abortifacients, and sterilization in its insurance packets.

Religious Liberty Is a Catch-22

At this point in the argument, if I were in the public square or even more a public university, I would no doubt be treated to shouts of "Fascist!" and, among the more historically-minded, "Torquemada!" [Tomás de, prominent leader of the Spanish Inquisition]. In other words, my "freedom of speech" would be pummeled in the name of what appears to be freedom of religion because I seem to be implying, by calling into question the unalienable right to believe whatever one wants, that I intend to impose upon everyone else what *I* happen to believe.

That is so unspeakably bad, a kind of blasphemy, that he who dares even imply it, thereby forfeits one First Amendment guarantee (freedom of speech), for the protection of another more sacred (everyone else's free exercise of religion).

That is precisely why we need a secular state to protect us, so that one man's religious beliefs aren't allowed to lord it over everyone or anyone else's.

And *that* ends us back at the puzzler: the affirmation of religious liberty leads to the suppression of religion by a secular state. The secular state is thereby empowered to impose unbelief, including the particular moral beliefs held dearly by secularism. The affirmation of religious liberty leads to its extinction at the hands of the secular state.

This seems to work so well for the cause of secularization, landing us right back under the thumb of a secular and secularizing government, that we have warrant to ask a more-than-interesting question: Is that the *way* it's been designed to work? More provocatively, was it designed to work that way by secularists, i.e., those who wished to subtract Christianity from public dominance and replace it with secularism?

Religious Diversity Encouraged

It's worth exploring, beginning with Thomas Jefferson's provocative words, written in a letter to [Jewish medical doctor] Jacob De La Motta (1820), that seem to imply that maximizing the diversity of religious beliefs keeps any one of them from gaining control of political power. For Jefferson, "religious freedom is the most effectual anodyne [pain remedy] against religious dissension: the maxim of civil government being reversed in that of religion, where its true form is 'divided we stand, united, we fall.'" The greater the diversity of beliefs, the less likely any of them will have enough strength to gain political power. And so, as far as religious beliefs go, "divided we stand."

This same approach would appear to be spelled out more directly in James Madison's famous Federalist [Paper #]10, dealing with the danger of factions. The problem with factions is, for Madison, that there are generally *too few* of them. With a mere handful of factions, each "united and actuated by some common impulse of passion," it is all too easy for one of these factions to swell to a majority and gain political ascendancy. Once having gained its position of power, it can then steer the republic in its own particular direction. The cure is to continually stir up *more* factions, especially from the national level. And Madison makes clear this principle applies to religion. While "in particular states . . . a religious sect may degenerate into a political faction in a part of the confederacy . . . the variety of sects dispersed over the entire face of it [i.e., the nation], must secure the national councils against any danger from that source . . ." In strategic sum, the more sects, the better, and so wise leaders will encourage religious faction.

Religious Liberty Leads to Plurality

This raises an almost impossibly delicate question about James Madison, the father of the Bill of Rights, and hence the First Amendment. Is the affirmation of the *right* of every man to believe whatever he wants—religious liberty understood in the way that Madison expresses it in his "Memorial and Remonstrance"—a way to promote a greater number of Christian sectarian factions, so that none of them will, by majority rule, be able to gain control of the national government?

I am not just asking the relatively benign question, "Does the free exercise clause help to keep any one Christian sect from attempting to establish itself as the national church?" The obvious answer would have to be "yes."

I am asking the more delicate, even explosive question: Did Jefferson and Madison believe that maximum religious plurality was something the national government should actively promote?

Or, put more pointedly: Is Christian unity—prayed for by Jesus Christ, "for those who believe in me . . . that they may be one" (John 17:20–21)—precisely the thing that the state must both fear and seek to undermine at every turn?

Is, then, the affirmation of religious liberty, defined as the right to believe whatever one wants, a kind of "divide and conquer" strategy, one that continually and quite purposefully undermines the essential Christian goal of unity?

I think there is reason to answer both "Yes" and "No," and both answers will help Christians defend themselves from current attempts by the secular state to extinguish the church and its public influence.

Private, Individual Belief

To understand more fully how the affirmation of religious liberty, or more exactly, the right to believe whatever one wants, was designed as a strategy of divide and conquer we'd have to go back beyond Jefferson and Madison to Benedict Spinoza, the great 17th century radical Enlightenment thinker.

It's beyond the scope of this article to delve deeply into Spinoza, but as an overview we can say the following. Spinoza was one of the first great modern freethinkers, an atheist or a pantheist (depending on how one cashes out his assertion that "God is nature, and nature is God"). In either case, he was a devout enemy of Christianity and his own Judaism, devoted to his own reason against the dictates of any revealed religion because the latter (so he believed) was derived from the foolishness of irrational superstition.

The great problem for Spinoza was what has been called the theological-political problem: tersely put, in all societies the many religious fools lord it over the few enlightened philosophers. This was the problem he set himself out to solve in his famous *Theological-Political Treatise.*

His solution, as you may have guessed, was to assert the absolute right by nature of everyone to believe anything he wants. Or to put it in its proper political setting—and here we note that Spinoza is rightly held to be the father of modern political liberalism—each person has the natural right to believe whatever he wants as long as he is publicly law-abiding. Belief is private; morality is public. One has the right to believe anything one wants about God, as long as one behaves (and especially ceases to bother others about their beliefs).

A Two-Fold, Intended Effect

Spinoza's solution had a two-fold, intended effect. First, it flattered the "fools" by ascribing to each one of them the extraordinary right to define God as they each saw fit. Second, it shielded Spinoza himself, an atheist or pantheist, from public persecution by Christians. In the liberal state as he defined and designed it, Spinoza, too, had the absolute right to define his own beliefs.

But to return to our previous point, the affirmation of this right would effectively multiply the number of different beliefs accordingly. The more deeply each person affirmed his own right to define his own religion, the more religions there would be. The more individually-constructed religions, the more each would consider it essential to protect this right, thereby empowering the liberal state to ensure that each person's private beliefs were protected from assault by others' beliefs. The ultimate result, after some churning, would be a secular, liberal state, one defined by no one's beliefs and hence by *unbelief*.

Played out in this way, Spinoza's atheism becomes the default "belief" of the liberal state. Or, we might say, unbelief has become the established belief, the established religion.

Jefferson and Madison are, arguably, heirs to that strategy, although as Deists their established belief was gotten as the result of the subtraction of Trinitarianism leaving the remainder of Unitarianism. Not as radical as Spinoza, but leaning in that direction. Historically, our liberal state has now gone beyond the wan Deism of these founders, and is pushing toward the

Liberals Are Dismantling Religious Liberty

The "ministerial exception" to employment discrimination law, affirmed 9–0 by the Supreme Court in the *Hosanna-Tabor* case in January 2012, will be no protection at all, since there is no way to shoehorn all these roles and functions into that exceptions category, no matter how broadly "minister" is defined. But to date, there is no state that has seen fit to accommodate the religious conscience even of avowedly religious ministries in this respect, let alone the consciences of religious persons doing business in the for-profit and nonprofit sectors.

Matthew J. Franck, Public Discourse, *June 18, 2013. www.thepublicdiscourse.com.*

complete secularist unbelief that has already been firmly established in Europe's liberal democracies. Spinoza won out.

Invented by the Church

Here, too, we've got a much longer story that would have to be conveyed to fully understand the point, but in overview we can recover an older sense of religious liberty which actually affirms the unity of the church, rather than dismantling it by dividing it into ever smaller splinters.

It will surprise readers, perhaps, to find out that what we call the "separation of church and state" was actually invented *by the church*. And not recently, either. The principled distinction between the church and political power was something hammered out by the church between the 5th and 12th centuries.

Ecclesiastical and political power—or priestly and royal, as they called it—must be kept distinct because each has its own specific function, and each becomes corrupted by trying to usurp the function of the other. The church deals with the eternal fate of the soul, and state with the temporal cares of this world. When the church usurps political power, it becomes worldly and corrupt, using its spiritual resources for mere political ends. When the state usurps the domain of the church, it uses spiritual power as an instrument for political gain, bending doctrines to suit its worldly goals and engaging in endless political simony and nepotism. For the good of each, the church and state must keep to their own proper domains.

Free from Political Manipulation

The reforming popes during this period pushed this distinction between church and state largely because they were combating the various attempts by Christian kings, emperors, dukes, and other land lords to subordinate the church to their political aims, as in, for example, the widespread custom of kings and lesser land holders appointing priests and abbots of their own choosing, or of treating the churches on their lands as a ready source of tithe revenue, or even of meddling in doctrine. The church must be independent of—free from—such manipulation.

And that is the proper, original declaration of religious liberty: the right of the church to be free from manipulations by the state.

Note that this is a very different thing from the notion that each of us has a right to define our belief in God any way we fancy. It is a freedom from state interference or control so that the church—the unified church—can go about its work, the care of souls.

A Difference of Definition

In a secondary, but very important sense, it is the freedom of the state as well. The freedom of the state not to be turned into a theocracy with priests ruling as kings, the freedom of the state not to be turned into a monastery with the most stringent demands for holiness imposed on everyone by political force, the freedom of the state to govern the things of this world according to the best dictates of the virtue of prudence, the freedom of the state from having to settle doctrines and doctrinal disagreements.

But doesn't this last freedom—the freedom of the state from having to settle doctrines and doctrinal disagreements—somehow land us back in the puzzler, with the secular liberal state imposing non-belief?

No, there is a very big difference, all the difference, in declaring that the state should keep out of doctrinal quarrels (a prohibition of state power), and declaring that the state should impose unbelief by actively removing all vestiges of Christianity from our civilization (a positive mandate, of which the HHS mandate is a living example).

Or, more deeply, there is all the difference, between defining religious liberty as the right of the unified church to be free from manipulations by the state, and defining religious liberty as the right of every individual to believe whatever he wants, which destroys the unity of the church and leaves the individual powerless before the manipulations of the state.

> *"The last people anyone needs to fear on religious liberty are Christian conservatives, who are its strongest guardians."*

Conservative Politics Protect Religious Liberty

David Limbaugh

In the following viewpoint, David Limbaugh argues that liberals are destroying religious liberty in their attempts to defend it. He contends that public officials can and should use their "worldview," or religious beliefs, when making policy decisions and that this does not threaten the religious liberty of others. Limbaugh concludes that Christian conservatives do more to protect religious liberty than liberals do. David Limbaugh is a lawyer, political commentator, syndicated columnist, best-selling author, and the brother of talk-show host Rush Limbaugh.

As you read, consider the following questions:

1. According to Limbaugh, how are liberals damaging religious liberty?

2. What are the three parts of Reagan conservatism advocated by Limbaugh?

3. According to the author, what did Rick Santorum say about the free exercise clause of the First Amendment?

The First Amendment to the United States Constitution contains two clauses addressing religious liberty: "Congress shall make no law respecting an establishment of religion, or prohibiting the free exercise thereof."

It's a shame that in their modern misguided zeal to read the first clause as mandating a complete separation of church and state, liberals do great damage to the second clause and defeat the overarching purpose of both: ensuring religious liberty.

Ever since the so-called Christian right began its organized activism during the 1980s, liberals (and some others) have become increasingly nervous about (and critical of) Christian influence in politics, let alone the public square.

This issue has reared its controversial head during the [2012] Republican presidential primary because of candidate Rick Santorum's unashamed and outspoken commitment to his Catholic faith and Christian values. It's not just leftists who are complaining; many on the right are, as well.

Republicans Must Unite

For years, there has been an uneasy alliance inside the Republican "big tent," between those who embrace social conservatism and those who would just as soon see it deleted from the party platform. With our anxiety about the national debt, economic issues are naturally at the forefront of people's concerns. Some believe that those who are still articulating social issues in this period of crisis are at least annoying and possibly detrimental to the cause of electing a Republican who can build a wide enough coalition to defeat the primary culprit in America's race to bankruptcy: President Barack Obama.

I think it's a false choice to say that we conservatives must pick between economic issues and social ones. It's also a mistake to believe there is a clear dichotomy between economic conservatives and social conservatives. As I've written before, [President Ronald] Reagan conservatism is a three-legged stool—economic, social and national defense issues—and the three are compatible and probably embraced by most Republicans.

Our center-right tent is big enough to include libertarians, economic conservatives who either are indifferent to social issues or consider themselves socially liberal, and so-called neoconservatives, who tend to emphasize national defense issues over the other two—although they might reject that characterization. We all must unite to defeat President Obama.

Public Religious Expression

But with Santorum's rise in the polls, many are expressing their anxiety about his perceived religiosity and are depicting him as a threat to religious liberty.

Some are abuzz about his interview [in February 2012] with [journalist] George Stephanopoulos on ABC's [television show] "This Week," in which Santorum stated that he does not believe separation of church and state is absolute. He stated that the First Amendment's free exercise clause guarantees that the church and its members have as much right to try to influence policy as anyone else. And he's absolutely correct.

Not only are the words "separation of church and state" not contained in the Constitution but this phrase from Thomas Jefferson's letter to the Danbury Baptists does not mean what many people say it does.

The First Amendment's establishment clause says that Congress shall not establish a national church, because the Framers didn't want the government telling us whom or how to worship. Their overarching concern, then, was protecting religious liberty. The free exercise clause also strengthens the religious freedom guarantee.

The point is that both clauses are dedicated to religious liberty, and neither purports to ban religious expression from the public square or from the mouths of public officials.

No matter how expansively one reads the First Amendment's establishment clause, no one, including Jefferson, would have made the ludicrous argument that presidents (or other public officials) must leave their worldview at the door of the White House and govern apart from it, as if that would be possible. Advocating policy positions based on one's worldview is light-years away from establishing—or even supporting—a national religion.

Trying to Quash Religious Liberty

Christian conservatives are not the ones demonstrating intolerance and threatening the freedoms of religion and religious expression. They would never consider being so presumptuous and tyrannical as to try to silence those who disagree with them, ban them from the public square, or advance the spurious argument that they are not entitled to advocate policies based on their worldview.

Ironically, it is probably the secular left that is most responsible for the dramatic rise and persistent influence of the Christian political right in politics, with their gross judicial activism in abortion jurisprudence and their judicial tyranny coercing states to accept same-sex marriage against the will of the people. They are the ones who demonize as "homophobes" and "bigots" those seeking to preserve traditional marriage. Christian conservatives don't try to shut them up, but many are now trying to shut us up—through the specious application of the First Amendment, no less.

The last people anyone needs to fear on religious liberty are Christian conservatives, who are its strongest guardians.

Above all others, they will fight to preserve everyone's right to express and practice his religion or non-religion as he pleases.

> "The campaign to redefine 'religious liberty' aims not simply to win religious exemptions to the law, but to contest the authority of secular law itself."

Conservatives' Use of Religious Liberty as a Political Issue Threatens Democracy

Jay Michaelson

In the following viewpoint, Jay Michaelson discusses how the Christian Right has co-opted the term religious liberty *as a rationale for discrimination by persons holding certain religious beliefs. He argues that this conservative campaign is well organized, well funded, and making progress in getting policies changed to suit the religious conservative agenda. Michaelson concludes that social justice advocates need to present a more organized opposition to this campaign. Jay Michaelson is an attorney, author, activist, and religious liberty fellow at Political Research Associates, a social justice think tank.*

As you read, consider the following questions:

1. According to Michaelson, how have religious conservatives reframed the debate over religious liberty?

Jay Michaelson, "Executive Summary," *Redefining Religious Liberty: The Covert Campaign Against Civil Rights*, March 2013, pp. 10–12. Copyright © 2013 by Political Research Associates. All rights reserved. Reproduced by permission.

2. What percentage of Americans believe that religious liberty is threatened, according to a June 2012 survey cited by Michaelson?

3. What is the Christian Right's endgame in the battle over religious liberty, according to the author?

A highly active, well-funded network of conservative Roman Catholic intellectuals and evangelicals are waging a vigorous challenge to LGBTQ [lesbian, gay, bisexual, transgender, queer] and reproductive rights by charging that both threaten their right-wing definition of "religious liberty." The Christian Right campaign to redefine "religious liberty" has been limiting women's reproductive rights for more than a decade and has recently resulted in significant religious exemptions from antidiscrimination laws, same-sex marriage laws, policies regarding contraception and abortion, and educational policies. Religious conservatives have succeeded in reframing the debate, inverting the victim-oppressor dynamic, and broadening support for their agenda.

While the religious liberty debate is a growing front in the ongoing culture wars, it is actually an old argument repurposed for a new context. In the postwar era, the Christian Right defended racial segregation, school prayer, public religious displays, and other religious practices that infringed on the liberties of others by claiming that restrictions on such public acts infringed upon their religious liberty. Then as now, the Christian Right turned antidiscrimination arguments on their heads: instead of African Americans being discriminated against by segregated Christian universities, the universities were being discriminated against by not being allowed to exclude them; instead of public prayers oppressing religious minorities, Christians are being oppressed by not being able to offer them.

Circumventing Secular Law

In the "religious liberty" framework, the Christian Right attacks access to contraception, access to abortion, same-sex marriage, and antidiscrimination laws—not on moral grounds (e.g., that contraception is morally wrong or that LGBTQ rights violate "family values") but because they allegedly impinge upon the religious freedoms of others (e.g., by forcing employers to violate their religion by providing contraception coverage).

The nerve center of the conservative "religious liberty" campaign is a small group of conservative Roman Catholic intellectuals and scholars concentrated around the Becket Fund for Religious Liberty, a public interest law firm based in Washington, D.C., and the United States Conference of Catholic Bishops (USCCB). Anthony Picarello, former counsel of the Becket Fund, left in 2007 to serve as USCCB's general counsel to work against marriage equality. These Roman Catholic organizations are supported by conservative evangelical allies, including organizations such as the Alliance Defending Freedom, Christian Legal Society, and Family Research Council. These alliances were forged in the antichoice movement, which has provided strong turnout of supporters at "religious liberty" events. These alliances were expressed in the Manhattan Declaration, which launched in 2009 when 150 Roman Catholic and evangelical clergy signed a statement to defend "life, marriage and religious liberty." Examination of these affiliations, history, and current activities makes clear that the campaign to redefine "religious liberty" aims not simply to win religious exemptions to the law, but to contest the authority of secular law itself.

Subverting Basic Human Rights

The conservative "religious liberty" campaign's methods include:

- conducting a PR [public relations] campaign to convince Americans that religious liberty is under attack and deploying misleading exaggerations to scare voters, for instance, by falsely claiming that churches will be required to sacralize same-sex weddings and employers forced to pay for abortions;

- reframing questions of discrimination (e.g., in the Boy Scouts) as questions of the religious liberty of those who wish to discriminate;

- filing lawsuits to limit LGBTQ rights on religious liberty grounds and exploiting ambiguities in the law to conduct a nationwide litigation campaign;

- exploiting the structural ambiguity in civil rights law that emerges when fundamental rights clash, as that between religious expression and civil rights;

- scaring the public by eliding the differences in legal standards between discrimination against LGBTQ people and discrimination against African Americans and other racial minorities, and suggesting that protections for the latter will be extended to the former;

- influencing legislation to obtain exemptions from anti-discrimination laws, and enabling Christian organizations to discriminate (e.g., student clubs in the Virginia university system);

- limiting access to reproductive health care, first through a series of religious exemptions for abortion and now by attempting to limit insurance coverage for contraceptives under the federal Affordable Care Act;

- attempting to expand existing religious exemptions beyond religious organizations to include private businesses (such as the retailer Hobby Lobby, the plaintiff in a prominent current case); and

- marshaling the support of influential academics such as Douglas Laycock, a distinguished professor at the University of Virginia Law School who successfully argued a key religious liberty case before the U.S. Supreme Court for the Becket Fund, and longtime conservative Catholic campaigner Robert P. George of Princeton University, who was coauthor of the Manhattan Declaration and is a board member of the Becket Fund. They and other scholars provide intellectual leadership for the movement, both within the Christian Right and more broadly.

Increasingly Visible

The "religious liberty" campaign's influence on contemporary politics and debate is increasingly visible. For example:

- It was a significant topic in the 2012 vice-presidential debate;

- It was the Christian Right's primary argument opposing same-sex marriage in the North Carolina, Minnesota, and Maine ballot initiatives in the fall of 2012;

- The Ethics and Public Policy Center in Washington D.C. is developing religious liberty caucuses in state legislatures to promote the Christian Right public policy agenda opposing LGBTQ and reproductive rights (At least nine states currently have such caucuses);

- The conservative "religious liberty" argument has been instrumental in winning exemptions from same-sex marriage laws and reducing women's access to contraception coverage;

- While a June 2012 survey by the Public Religion Research Institute found only 39 percent of Americans believe religious freedom is threatened, polls also show the argument is effective when the Right sows confusion among the public; for instance, in suggesting that ministers would be forced to marry LGBTQ couples if a state legalizes same-sex marriage.

Creating a Christian Nation

Aside from its power in legal arguments, the Right's "religious liberty" claims appeal to both conservative and moderate Christians by resonating with core martyrdom and persecution narratives. Moreover, among Roman Catholics, it resonates with the memory of Protestant separationists' anti-Catholicism; among moderates, it resonates with the American civic value of religious freedom. Finally, the Right's "religious liberty" arguments have won intellectual respectability even among some liberals. Unlike the Christian Right's usual claims, grounded in religious dogma, the conservative "religious liberty" argument appeals to liberal values enshrined in the Constitution and has the support of respected academics. Liberals may support many of these "religious liberty" causes and key players in the campaign to redefine religious liberty—such as the Becket Fund—have litigated in defense of Muslims as well as Christians. And there is a strong popular appeal to some basic arguments; after all, few want to abridge religious freedom.

Yet there should be no mistake: the Right's "religious liberty" campaign is a key front in the broader culture war designed to fight the same social battles on new-sounding terms, and is part of a movement with old roots in Christian Dominionism (a form of theocracy) and ties to conservative Catholics who launched the antichoice movement. Its deliberate, inversion of victim-oppressor dynamic has led to limits on women's and LGBTQ people's real freedoms in the name of defending chimerical [fantasy] ones. Proponents may sincerely believe that they are defending religious freedom, but the campaign's endgame is a "Christian nation" defined in exclusively conservative terms. And it is thus far inadequately opposed.

Liberals Need to Be Better Organized

To contest the Right's "religious liberty" argument, social justice forces must publicize the existence of a coordinated campaign to redefine religious liberty, support a faith-based response to it, counter common misinformation, contest the rhetorical frame of "religious liberty," foster robust academic responses, and take a pro-active rather than reactive political role. Specifically, this report recommends that social justice advocates:

1. Define and Publicize the Coordinated Campaign to Redefine Religious Liberty.

While grassroots evangelicals are active in the conservative "religious liberty" campaign against LGBTQ and reproductive rights, it is a coordinated fight led by well-established right-wing institutions like the Becket Fund and Alliance Defending Freedom. The Roman Catholic Church hierarchy and conservative Catholics are important thought leaders for the campaign. The evangelical/Roman Catholic alliance builds on relationships forged in the antichoice movement.

2. Organize a Unified Response

There is need for further mapping, coordinating, and building out alliances among advocates countering the Right's campaign. We need to strengthen the alliance between prochoice and LGBTQ forces, and ally with emerging faith-based responses. Alliances must also be made with liberal business owners and libertarians; this can increase the effectiveness of existing efforts.

3. Counter Misinformation

Many conservative "religious liberty" claims rely on falsehoods and scare tactics. Simply put, clergy will never be forced to perform a same-sex marriage. Social justice advocates must learn and be able to counter the Right's go-to examples of spurious "religious liberty" violations. Understanding and clarifying the Right's use of the martyr narrative and inversion of the victim-oppressor dynamic is a good start to countering right-wing rhetoric.

4. Reclaim the Religious Liberty Frame

The term "religious liberty," like the phrase "family values," has become a code for the larger culture wars. While religious belief and expression are valid and protected constitutional claims, religious liberty is not the freedom to discriminate and harm others. It does not allow a boss to tell an employee what health care they can obtain, taking away the employee's ability to make moral and religious choices. Nor does sexual and gender equality have to be pitted against religious liberty. The clash is not just between secularism and religion, or equality and religion, but of competing religious values. Challenging the conservative frame also means distinguishing between commercial and religious acts, and valuing competing civil rights; an effective response requires sustained intellectual and legal challenges to the Right's argument.

5. Develop Academic Responses

Social justice advocates must take seriously the influence of right-wing academics on policy and public debate. Religious freedom is a complex topic, which can too often become co-opted by the conservative "religious liberty" campaign. That this happens, often unknowingly, to fair-minded academics and legal scholars is something that can be reversed by raising awareness of the issue, including with academic conferences on the topic.

6. Leverage Religious Communities

We must build on existing interfaith work to counter the conservative "religious liberty" narrative, informing and organizing more in faith communities. The social justice community must create unity by issuing a common "Call to Conscience" of religious people seeking to maintain their religious liberty against the conservative proposals and policies. LGBTQ faith communities, Jewish and progressive faith organizations, in particular, must be supported in countering the Right's claims about what religious liberty means.

7. Ongoing Research and Monitoring

Social justice advocates and defenders of true religious freedom must become better informed about the right-wing campaign to redefine religious liberty—including its principal players, strategies, and vulnerabilities. Ongoing investigative research into U.S. conservatives' use of religious liberty legal and rhetorical strategies, both domestically and abroad, is needed to keep advocates and journalists informed about strategically significant developments. Moreover, we must track the influence of conservative academics on policy and public debate.

| "It is absolutely discriminatory to allow the beliefs of employers to violate those of employees."

Religion and Politics Must Remain Separate to Preserve Religious Liberty

Sara Hutchinson

In the following viewpoint, Sara Hutchinson expresses opposition to the US Conference of Catholic Bishops (USCCB) for its blatantly discriminatory treatment of people in the name of religious liberty. She contends that the heart of the problem is that the USCCB thinks that institutions should have rights of conscience and therefore the ability to discriminate against their employees or members on the basis of that so-called conscience. Sara Hutchinson is the domestic program director for Catholics for Choice, an organization that supports women's rights in matters of sexuality and reproductive health.

As you read, consider the following questions:

1. According to Hutchinson, is the fight over federally mandated contraceptive access about religious liberty or reproductive rights?

2. According to the author, what right does the USCCB believe it should receive in return for the good it does in some parts of society?

3. How many groups are involved with the Coalition for Liberty and Justice, according to Hutchinson?

In their campaign against certain provisions of the Affordable Care Act, the United States Conference of Catholic Bishops has claimed that their right to religious liberty eclipsed others' right to contraceptive access. Others have argued that this was not a debate about religious freedom at all—it was simply about reproductive rights.

Both sides are wrong. There is a real debate to have about religious freedom, but it's not the one that the bishops want it to be. Some of the pertinent questions include: Are there any circumstances in which certain groups may be denied health-care services for religious reasons? What privileges, if any, should service providers demand from the government?

A broad spectrum of organizations has come together as the Coalition for Liberty & Justice because, as both secular and religious groups, we oppose efforts by conservative religious advocates to restrict individuals' ability to access a wide variety of services under the banner of religious freedom.

With the launch of its Ad Hoc Committee on Religious Liberty last September [2011], the United States Conference of Catholic Bishops (USCCB) was transparent about the future it was working towards. If the bishops get their way, hardworking families will not be able to afford contraception; with a shrinking safety net, more children will grow up in poverty. Victims of sex trafficking will not receive unbiased counseling and will endure a forced pregnancy. Lesbian, gay and transgender people will be refused jobs and services; committed couples will be denied the rights and benefits of marriage. Men and women won't be able to get their prescriptions filled if their employer or pharmacist judges the use of the medicine immoral. People at risk of contracting or spreading HIV won't learn that condoms can help save their lives and the lives of people they love. Women who need abortions, even to save their lives, will be turned away. This is not what Americans want, and it's not what America is at its foundation.

Employers Should Not Meddle

Last year [2011], Catholics for Choice heard one American's story, that of a teacher at a Catholic school in the Midwest, whom we'll call "Sandra." This young woman had taken a pay cut to do the type of work she loved, but found out at the pharmacy counter that her new insurance plan did not cover birth control. Paying out-of-pocket for the contraceptive method that worked best for her, a non-generic prescription, was a significant strain on the budget she had carefully planned with her husband. Sandra especially objected to the interference in her personal decision-making about contraception: "I don't like being told by some guy that I've never met that I can't use it."

Sandra and employees at all other "religious institutions" should be granted an equal opportunity to access affordable contraception. Ensuring such access avoids the untenable position of allowing the government to determine which employees' consciences—and health—matter, simply on the basis of where they work. But what we're hearing from the USCCB is that these women's ability to make moral decisions for themselves doesn't matter. The conscience of people like Sandra may be run over by an employer or bishop, and that would be acceptable collateral damage.

An Orwellian Coup

That the bishops would have convinced anyone that their version of "religious freedom" is anything but oppression represents an Orwellian coup. The writer George Orwell paid close attention to anyone, from politicians to businesspeople, who spoke in jargon because he said "if thought corrupts language, language can also corrupt thought." In this way, a crusade has been whipped up by sweeping calls to defend religious liberty from its enemies, when the stakes and even the players have been depicted incorrectly. The USCCB would have us believe that a school, a Taco Bell or a hospital has a "conscience" and "freedom of religion." They do not. Individuals, according to our Catholic tradition, have consciences and deserve to exercise them without coercion. Individuals also deserve to have their freedom of and freedom from religion protected.

There is a natural give-and-take that is expected from members of a society. We "give" money from our insurance premiums for coverage of many medical services that we may not agree with or need ourselves, and expect to avail ourselves of that safety net when we need it. The institutional Catholic church, for its part, benefits from a tax-preferred status and has a long history of seeking government funding streams— including support for Catholic schools, hospitals and programs run by Catholic Charities, which give back to the community. But just as institutions do not have a conscience, they are not citizens. Individuals have a conscience, and they enjoy citizenship. The only "second-class citizens" created by laws allowing employers to refuse contraceptive coverage are women. It is absolutely discriminatory to allow the beliefs of employers to violate those of employees. But the bishops want to rewrite several important parts of our American social contract.

In the laundry list the bishops laid out last September, we see that the false idea of institutional conscience is a handy excuse for preventing same-sex couples from adopting, or victims of human trafficking from accessing comprehensive reproductive healthcare. The same reasoning is used to justify keeping the person living in rural Africa with no local access to condoms from protecting herself from the spread of HIV. The USCCB believes it has a right to receive government funding to provide religiously circumscribed services here and

Church and Government Work Best Separately

It seems that the failure to separate church and state hurts religion. Why is that? Here's the answer: Freedom and competition are good for religion. When houses of worship are dependent on government for support, religion loses its vitality. In America, religious groups rely on voluntary contributions. This policy makes them more robust.

Church-state separation also guarantees the right of religious groups to speak out on issues of justice, ethics and morality. In countries where religion receives tax support, clergy usually are wary of criticizing the government. After all, they don't want to bite the hand that feeds them! Because religious groups in America are truly independent, they feel no such constraints. They are free to try to persuade other Americans toward their perspective.

Americans United for Separation of Church and State,
"America's Legacy of Religious Liberty—Pass It On."
www.au.org.

abroad, and claims that the good that it does in some sectors of society gives it license to discriminate at taxpayer expense in others. It's a cold kind of brinksmanship that puts too many individuals' freedom in the balance.

Liberals Are Gathering in Support

The bishops' misrepresentation of religious freedom has brought together a remarkable coalition of diverse groups who are all on the same page. Can you imagine sitting at one table with feminists, atheists, progressive Catholics, rabbis, gay

Catholics, sexual and reproductive health nonprofits, as well as groups from the medical and legal fields? Representatives from each of these fields make up the Coalition for Liberty & Justice, and each advocacy organization serves a different community. There are those keeping an eye on the separation of church and state. Medical and nursing students are looking to the care they want to provide for future patients. Advocates for LGBT [lesbian, gay, bisexual, and transgender] rights wish to prevent discrimination from being encoded into law by religious fiat. And religious groups across the board see that giving one ultraconservative sector of one faith special legal protections jeopardizes the freedom of worship for all people of faith. Everyone agrees that the most equitable solution to differing values lies in creating the minimum structures necessary to help provide services to individuals who want them. The coalition supports freedom of conscience—for individuals, including health-care providers and for service recipients, but not for institutions.

This wide variety of stakeholders has come together precisely because this debate means a lot of things to a lot of different people. The bishops have denied that their recent campaign against the regulation is about contraception, but for the everyday person who utilizes contraception, having affordable access to such services has many implications. No-cost contraception for the average woman, including many Catholic women, can mean following her religious beliefs, following her conscience, protecting her health, saving money for her family, protecting her future or myriad other things that we cannot be privy to. If the bishops succeed in eliminating coverage, it will most definitely be about contraceptive access, and all of the things that access means to millions of Americans. Each of the other items on the bishops' religious freedom wish list has similar concrete effects on real people.

In contrast to some of the contentious debate we've heard about religious freedom recently, working with the Coalition for Liberty & Justice has been a reminder that civil society is actually supposed to be civil. Nonprofits serving different constituencies don't have to be in competition. Rather, groups that are secure enough in their values that they can listen to others' differing perspectives are free to share resources, which can be taken home to their stakeholders and translated into more capacity and deeper wisdom. Catholics for Choice approached Nancy Kaufman from the National Council of Jewish Women as co-convener in this spirit, and now, joined by more than 50 additional organizations, we are realizing the benefits of identifying commonalities among the differences of our backgrounds.

For us as Catholics, social justice is at the core of our faith. We are compelled by our religious tradition to work toward justice and equity for all and to create a society in which women and men, young and old, poor and rich are treated with the same dignity and respect and granted the same opportunity. As Catholics, our tradition of social justice informs everything we do and defines how we relate to family members, neighbors, coworkers and our fellow Americans. It requires us to stand with those who are the neediest—the hungry, the homeless, the jobless—and then help to fill their needs.

Each of the coalition's members has traveled distinct paths to get here, but we have arrived at the same conclusion: freedom of religion must translate into individual freedom of conscience, or it's not true freedom at all.

> "What we perceive as truth, how we frame morality and our vision for society are undeniably linked to our religious beliefs or lack thereof."

Separation of Religion and Politics Endangers Religious Liberty

David Green

In the following viewpoint, David Green contends that religion and politics are inextricably combined. He implores people to listen to each other and explains that trying to understand a different point of view does not compromise a person' own beliefs. Green concludes that peace can only be achieved if people come together in understanding. David Green is minister of the Amarillo Unitarian Universalist Fellowship in Amarillo, Texas.

As you read, consider the following questions:

1. According to Green, what foods do religion and politics resemble and why?

2. Why does Green compare political campaigns to "apocalyptic impulses"?

3. What can politics teach religion about working together constructively, according to the author?

One truth of the American experience is the intimate relationship between religion and politics. Many claim our nation's founders always intended our republic to reflect certain religious values, while others insist quite the opposite.

Both sides of this argument are adept at quoting long-marbleized statesmen to prove their case. The opposing camps are unlikely to come to any consensus on the matter, not that they really want to. It's apparently more fun—and profitable—to disagree. . . .

Religion and Politics Are Complementary

The obvious reality is religion and politics share the same menu of public life and always have. They are our cultural peas and carrots—we go ahead and eat them in the same bite whether we prefer the taste of one over the other.

Many long and sleep-inducing history lectures explain how this came to pass, but I've come to the conclusion our religious and political beliefs and behaviors originate in the same cul-de-sac of our brains.

Watching a political convention on TV, one is struck by how closely it resembles a tent revival. Otherwise rational folks bounce and weep ecstatically, wave hands in the air, and shout "Amen!" Candidates—mere mortals—are endowed with saviorlike qualities by the adoring throng.

Like many expressions of faith, political campaigns often appeal to our apocalyptic impulses, the notion that the end of life as we know it will result if the other side wins.

Prophecies of doom produce much hand-wringing, moaning, gnashing of teeth and other scripturally-inspired expressions of angst. Opponents demonize one another to the extent we're led to expect catastrophe regardless of who comes out on top.

© Paul Fell/pfen314/CartoonStock.com.

Politicians know to push the buttons on our deepest fears and beliefs as the most effective method of energizing voters. Cutting to the heart of our emotions wins elections; appealing to rationality alone is the sure road to defeat. Not that faith is purely about emotion and absent of reason, but we'd be dishonest to pretend our faith is disconnected from our feelings.

Beliefs Need Not Be Compromised

What we perceive as truth, how we frame morality and our vision for society are undeniably linked to our religious beliefs or lack thereof. We get quite attached and emotional about such things. It makes perfect sense for those beliefs to inform our political sensibilities. There's no right or wrong to that; it just is.

It's also important to remember that just as firmly we might hold to our beliefs, in our free society there are plenty of others who will disagree with us, equally certain of the validity of their own convictions. That's always been true, so our choice is to behave as if we're engaged in a perpetual campaign of denigrating those others or get along with them.

I think I must be one of those rare birds who can see both sides of almost any argument. I have very good friends who occupy opposite points of the religious and political compass, placing me in a lonely mid-field position as they rush headlong toward each other from either end zone. My dream is to blow a whistle, call a time-out on all the self-righteous indignation and fruitless loathing and have everyone join hands for a chorus of "Kum-Bay-Ya." It's more likely I'll just get crushed in the middle.

Yet, I continue to hold onto a vision of people of different faith perspectives—no matter how staunchly held—awakening to the concept their beliefs need not be compromised by the mere act of listening to and seeking to understand the beliefs of others.

In politics, it's always instructive to witness after a long and brutal campaign how quickly the winners and losers kiss and make up, suddenly and miraculously rediscovering their civility. The vanquished may still believe the victor to be politically off the mark, but they still promise their support for the good of the whole. Both sides seem to understand in the real world of governing effectively, things like listening, understanding and compromise are actually how anything constructive ever gets done.

If that's the funny thing about politics, the same notion can lead to beautiful results when it comes to religion. We can understand one another not as contestants in a struggle to claim truth, but as fellow seekers of truly living together in peace.

Periodical and Internet Sources Bibliography

The following articles have been selected to supplement the diverse viewpoints presented in this chapter.

Gabriel Arana	"'Religious Liberty': The Next Big Front in the Culture Wars," *American Prospect*, November 8, 2013.
Judd Birdsall	"Os Guinness: Liberals and Conservatives Are Getting Religious Freedom Wrong," *Christianity Today*, August 2013.
Matthew Brown	"Religious Liberty Has Become a Call to Action for Conservatives," *Deseret News* (Salt Lake City, UT), August 3, 2013.
The Economist	"The Limits of Freedom and Faith; Religion and Human Rights," April 3, 2010.
Mary Ann Glendon	"First of Freedoms? How Religious Liberty Could Become a Second-Class Right," *America*, March 5, 2012.
Shahid Ali Panhwer and Maha Mussadaq	"Religion and Politics Must Not Mix in America, Experts Say," McClatchy DC, November 8, 2011. www.mcclatchydc.com.
Mike Sarzo	"Politics and Religion Should Stay Separate," Allvoices, September 23, 2013. www.allvoices.com.
Aaron Taylor	"Religious Liberty and the Rise of Conservative Liberalism," Ethika Politika September 12, 2013. http://ethikapolitika.org.
Matthew Tessnear	"Religious Freedom for All, or None?," *Shelby (NC) Star*, April 6, 2013.

For Further Discussion

Chapter 1

1. In her viewpoint, Jennifer A. Marshall argues that the separation of church and state is generally misunderstood. What does she claim that it really means?

2. In his viewpoint, Jay Michaelson argues that religious liberty advocates are really working to legalize discrimination. In his viewpoint, Ken Blackwell disagrees with Michaelson and contends that there is a real need to protect religious liberty in the United States. Which view do you agree with? Why?

3. In his viewpoint Charles J. Chaput states that the United States has strayed from the Founders' intentions regarding religious liberty. Do you agree or disagree? Why?

Chapter 2

1. In her viewpoint, Melissa Moschella argues that the HHS mandate violates the religious liberty of employers. Do you agree? Why or why not?

2. In his viewpoint, Tony Houston maintains that part of religious freedom in the United States is the right to believe in nothing at all. Do you agree or disagree? Why? Do you think it is okay for religious iconography to be placed in public spaces? Why or why not?

3. After reading the viewpoints by the Anti-Defamation League and the Alliance Defending Freedom, do you think prayer and religious expression have a place in public schools? Why or why not? Do you think reasonable accommodation could be made for students of many different faiths all attending the same school? Explain.

Chapter 3

1. In his viewpoint, Alan Sears contends that Obamacare violates the religious rights of business owners. How does it do that according to Sears? In his viewpoint, Barry W. Lynn argues that employers do not have the right to deny their employees access to birth control. Do you agree? Why or why not?

2. In his viewpoint, Conor Friedersdorf explains that the New York Police Department (NYPD) racially and ethnically profiled Muslims in an effort to combat terrorism. Do you think their efforts were justified? Why or why not? Does the fact that the NYPD never got any leads on terror activity and that no terrorism investigations were ever launched change your opinion? Explain your answer.

Chapter 4

1. After reading the viewpoint by Marta Cook and John Halpin, do you think that religious progressives are having as much of an impact during the twenty-first century as they did during the nineteenth and twentieth centuries? Why or why not? Cite examples in your answer.

2. According to David Limbaugh, why did the framers of the US Constitution write in the First Amendment that Congress shall not create a national church? Limbaugh describes Christian conservatives as the strongest guardians of religious liberty. What reason does he give for this description? Do you agree with him? Explain.

3. After reading the viewpoint by Sara Hutchinson, do you agree that institutions rather than individuals should be granted freedom of religion? Why or why not? Do you agree with David Greene that religion and politics are inseparable? Explain your answers and use examples from the viewpoints.

Organizations to Contact

The editors have compiled the following list of organizations concerned with the issues debated in this book. The descriptions are derived from materials provided by the organizations. All have publications or information available for interested readers. The list was compiled on the date of publication of the present volume; names, addresses, phone and fax numbers, and e-mail and Internet addresses may change. Be aware that many organizations take several weeks or longer to respond to inquiries, so allow as much time as possible.

Alliance Defending Freedom
15100 N. Ninetieth St., Scottsdale, AZ   85260
(800) 835-5233 • fax: (480) 444-0025
website: www.alliancedefendingfreedom.org

Founded in 1994, Alliance Defending Freedom is a Christian religious organization that works to change the US legal system to protect traditional Christian values, including religious liberty. Coordinating the efforts of more than two thousand lawyers and three hundred legal and policy organizations, Alliance Defending Freedom has won more than 80 percent of its court cases, including thirty-eight victories in the US Supreme Court. The organization's website provides information on the key issues that the group supports, ways people can get involved, and current and previous issues of its magazine, *Faith & Justice*.

American Civil Liberties Union (ACLU)
125 Broad St., 18th Fl., New York, NY   10004
(212) 549-2500
website: www.aclu.org

Founded in 1920, the American Civil Liberties Union is a national nonprofit, nonpartisan organization that works to defend and protect individual civil rights through court cases and legislation. The ACLU publishes several handbooks, public policy reports, project reports, civil liberties books, and pamphlets. The organization maintains a presence in every state in the United States, as well as in Puerto Rico and the District of Columbia.

Americans United for Separation of Church and State

1301 K St. NW, Ste. 850, East Tower, Washington, DC 20005
(202) 466-3234 • fax: (202) 466-2587
e-mail: americansunited@au.org
website: www.au.org

Founded in 1947, Americans United for Separation of Church and State is a nonprofit, nonpartisan, educational organization dedicated to maintaining the constitutional separation of church and state. It works in the courts, in Congress, and in state legislatures on a variety of issues, including school prayer, faith-based prison programs, prayer at government events, and workplace discrimination. It also publishes the magazine *Church & State*.

Baptist Joint Committee for Religious Liberty (BJC)

200 Maryland Ave. NE, Washington, DC 20002
(202) 544-4226 • fax: (202) 544-2094
e-mail: bjc@bjconline.org
website: www.bjconline.org

The Baptist Joint Committee for Religious Liberty is a Baptist advocacy and educational organization dedicated to defending religious liberty, protecting the separation of church and state, and promoting Baptist heritage. The BJC works within Washington, DC, to advocate its position to lawmakers and around the United States to educate people about religious liberty. The BJC website provides general information about religious liberty, including the free exercise of religion, public prayer, and religious displays. The site also offers a blog, relevant news stories, and links to sermons concerning freedom of religion.

The Becket Fund for Religious Liberty
3000 K St. NW, Ste. 220, Washington, DC   20007
(202) 955-0095 • fax: (202) 955-0090
e-mail: inquiries@becketfund.org
website: www.becketfund.org

Founded in 1994, the Becket Fund for Religious Liberty is a nonprofit legal group that seeks to protect the religious freedom of individuals of all faiths in the United States and abroad. The group also sponsors the Stanford Religious Liberty Clinic at Stanford University, which trains lawyers in religious liberty law. The Becket Fund website offers press releases, a blog, and regular updates on the group's legal casework.

Foundation for Individual Rights in Education (FIRE)
601 Walnut St., Ste. 510, Philadelphia, PA   19106
(215) 717-3473 • fax: (215) 717-3440
e-mail: fire@thefire.org
website: www.thefire.org

Founded in 1999, the Foundation for Individual Rights in Education is a nonprofit educational organization that works to defend the rights of students and faculty at universities and colleges in the United States. FIRE pursues its mission through litigation, campus projects, a network of shared resources, and an annual conference. On its website FIRE maintains a database of universities and colleges that provides a free-speech rating, news reports, FIRE cases, and FIRE blogs about each school. The website also offers information about different liberty issues, videos, podcasts, and various publications, including the quarterly newsletter *FIRE Quarterly*.

Freedom from Religion Foundation (FFRF)
PO Box 750, Madison, WI   53701
(608) 256-8900 • fax: (608) 204-0422
website: http://ffrf.org

Founded in 1978, the Freedom from Religion Foundation is a national nonprofit educational organization that works to protect the separation of church and state. The FFRF pursues its mission through litigation for separation of church and state violations; community outreach and education; an annual convention; a weekly radio show, *Freethought Radio*; and awards to public figures who speak plainly about religion. The FFRF also produces numerous books, brochures, and the twenty-page newspaper *Freethought Today*.

Religious Freedom Coalition

c/o William Murray, PO Box 77511, Washington, DC 20013
(202) 543-0300
website: www.religiousfreedomcoalition.org

The Religious Freedom Coalition is a nonprofit advocacy group that seeks to be the voice of conservatives and fights to preserve "America's Christian heritage." Issues the group supports include family values and voluntary public prayer; issues the group opposes include abortion, gay rights, and assisted suicide. The group pursues its goals by lobbying lawmakers, managing petition campaigns, and informing the public about legislative issues.

United States Commission on International Religious Freedom (USCIRF)

732 North Capitol St. NW, Ste. A714, Washington, DC 20401
(202) 523-3240 • fax: (202) 523-5020
e-mail: communications@uscirf.gov
website: www.uscirf.gov

The United States Commission on International Religious Freedom is an independent, bipartisan governmental commission dedicated to defending freedom of religion abroad. It watches for violations of religious freedom and makes policy recommendations to the president, the secretary of state, and the Congress. The USCIRF produces policy briefs, news reports, fact sheets, and a lengthy annual report that spotlights the conditions of many countries. These publications are available on the USCIRF website, along with press releases about the commission's work, a calendar of events, and a photo gallery.

Bibliography of Books

John M. Barry — *Roger Williams and the Creation of the American Soul: Church, State, and the Birth of Liberty.* New York: Penguin, 2012.

Jacques Berlinerblau — *How to Be Secular: A Call to Arms for Religious Freedom.* Boston: Houghton Mifflin Harcourt, 2012.

Marc O. DiGirolami — *The Tragedy of Religious Freedom.* Cambridge, MA: Harvard University Press, 2013.

Timothy M. Dolan — *True Freedom: On Protecting Human Dignity and Religious Liberty.* New York: Doubleday/Image, 2012.

Thomas F. Farr — *World of Faith and Freedom: Why International Religious Liberty Is Vital to American National Security.* New York: Oxford University Press, 2008.

Anthony Gill — *The Political Origins of Religious Liberty.* New York: Cambridge University Press, 2007.

Emily R. Gill — *An Argument for Same-Sex Marriage: Religious Freedom, Sexual Freedom, and Public Expressions of Civic Equality.* Washington, DC: Georgetown University Press, 2012.

Brian J. Grim and Roger Finke — *The Price of Freedom Denied: Religious Persecution and Conflict in the 21st Century.* New York: Cambridge University Press, 2011.

T. Jeremy Gunn
and John Witte

No Establishment of Religion: America's Original Contribution to Religious Liberty. New York: Oxford University Press, 2012.

Allen D. Hertzke, ed.

The Future of Religious Freedom: Global Challenge. New York: Oxford University Press, 2013.

Frank Lambert

Religion in American Politics: A Short History. Princeton, NJ: Princeton University Press, 2010.

Douglas Laycock

Overviews and History. Vol. 1 of *Religious Liberty.* Grand Rapids, MI: Eerdmans, 2010.

Brian Leiter

Why Tolerate Religion? Princeton, NJ: Princeton University Press, 2013.

Mark R. Levin

The Liberty Amendments: Restoring the American Republic. New York: Threshold, 2013.

David Niose

Nonbeliever Nation: The Rise of Secular Americans. New York: Palgrave Macmillan, 2012.

Lori Peek

Behind the Backlash: Muslim Americans After 9/11. Philadelphia: Temple University Press, 2011.

John Ragosta

Religious Freedom: Jefferson's Legacy, America's Creed. Charlottesville: University of Virginia Press, 2013.

Phyllis Schlafly
and George
Neumayr

No Higher Power: Obama's War on Religious Freedom. Washington, DC: Regnery, 2012.

| David Sehat | *The Myth of American Religious Freedom.* New York: Oxford University Press, 2010. |

| Timothy Shah and Matthew Franck | *Religious Freedom: Why Now? Defending an Embattled Human Right.* Princeton, NJ: Witherspoon Institute, 2012. |

| Arvind Sharma | *Problematizing Religious Freedom.* New York: Springer, 2011. |

| Winnifred Fallers Sullivan | *The Impossibility of Religious Freedom.* Princeton, NJ: Princeton University Press, 2011. |

| Kenneth D. Wald and Allison Calhoun-Brown | *Religion and Politics in the United States.* 6th ed. Lanham, MD: Rowman & Littlefield, 2010. |

| Steven Waldman | *Founding Faith: How Our Founding Fathers Forged a Radical New Approach to Religious Liberty.* New York: Random House, 2008. |

| Timothy Zick | *The Cosmopolitan First Amendment: Protecting Transborder Expressive and Religious Liberties.* New York: Cambridge University Press, 2013. |

Index

A

Abortion, 31, 32
    Catholic moral beliefs and, 42
    Christian right attacks, 158, 159, 160
    dangers of legalization, 127–131
    legal activism, 155
    medical beliefs in wrongfulness, 83
    restriction gains, 129
    societal accommodations, 84
    stance of American citizens, 168
    tax dollars spending, 108
Abortion-pill mandate, 107
Adams, John, 39
Addams, Jane, 137
Affordable Care Act
    Becket Fund lawsuits, 32
    birth control coverage debate, 106–107, 111–115, 160, 167
    description of coverage, 112–113
    religious exemption efforts, 31
    religious objections, 42, 107
    secular corporation non-exemptions, 113–115
AFP news agency report, 66–67
African Americans
    avoidance of police scrutiny, 120
    Christian right discrimination, 29, 31, 158, 160
    enslaved/deprivation of rights, 36
    president/presidential contender, 66
    Stop and Frisk policy, 117
Alliance Defending Freedom
    anti-LGBTQ campaign, 163
    representation of Christian businesses, 108–109, 113
    on school religious freedom, 94–101
    support for Catholic organizations, 159
American Center for Law and Justice, 113
American Muslims
    Becket Fund defense, 162
    conservative faction actions, 115
    fear of reprisals, 121, 122
    mosque-building rights, 66, 82
    support by Catholics, 80
    surveillance threats to religious liberty, 116–126
Anglicans, 56
Anti-bullying initiatives, 74
Anti-Defamation League, 86–93

B

Baker, Kevin, 124–125
Baptists, 56
Becket Fund for Religious Liberty
    anti-Affordable Care Act lawsuits, 32, 113
    anti-LGBTQ campaign, 163
    circumventing of secular law, 159
    filing of lawsuits, 32, 113
    opposition to Laycock, 30

potential liberal support, 162
US Supreme Court decision,
     161
Benedict XVI (Pope), 47, 129
Bill of Rights
   adoption, 56
   amendment issue, 70
   description/principles, 52–53,
      69, 74
   Madison, James, role, 142, 146
   ratification by states, 68
   See also Establishment Clause;
      Free-Exercise clause
Birth control, mandated
   religious liberty, nonviolation,
      111–115
   religious liberty, violation,
      106–110
*Bishop's Program of Social Recon-
   struction* (Ryan), 140
Blackwell, Ken, 34–37
Bloomberg, Michael, 118, 124–125
Bob Jones University, 29
Bradley, Gerard, 42
Bryan, William Jennings, 137
Bullies. *See* Religious liberty bul-
   lies

C

Cain, Herman, 66–67, 70
Carroll, Charles, 110
Carroll, John, 39
Catholic Charities, 30, 61, 82, 169
Catholic Relief Services (CRS), 83
Catholics/Catholic Church
   Affordable Care Act and, 30,
      107, 111–115, 160, 167
   anti-abortion campaign, 128
   anti-Catholic forces, 78
   evangelical comparison, 29

   right to religious liberty,
      79–82
   Second Vatican Council, 45,
      46–47, 52, 80
   social teachings, 137–139
   support for Jews, Mormons,
      Muslims, 80
   teachings, 46–47
   teachings/moral convictions,
      42
   treasuring of First Amend-
      ment, 79–80
   US settlements, 72
   weeding out religious impu-
      rity, 105
Center for Religious Liberty, 30
Chaput, Charles J., 38–43
China, religious-liberty violence,
   18
Christian business owners, 108–
   110
Christian conservatives
   agenda, 33
   birth control opposition, 113
   far-right Catholic coalition, 29
   protection of religious liberty,
      152–156
   same-sex marriage opposition,
      155–156
   Santorum, Rick, rise in polls,
      154
Christian Legal Society, 31, 159
Christian right
   attacks on religious liberty, 31,
      159
   claims of victim status, 29–30
   defense of racial segregation,
      158
   discrimination *vs.* African
      Americans, 29, 31, 158, 160
   opposition to LGBTQ equal-
      ity, 29

opposition to same-sex marriage, 161
origin, 29, 153
public policy agenda, 161
religious liberty goals, 158
same-sex marriage opposition, 29, 37, 155, 158, 159, 161
stance for right to discriminate, 29–30
See also Family Research Council
Christian Scientists, 75
Christianity
ancient Middle East communities, 46
belief in community, 40
early endorsements, by states, 68
faith-based deaths, 45
flight from Africa, 46
fundamentalist, 46, 113, 115
humanism basis, 53
Rauschenbusch, Walter, on purpose of, 138–139
stance against gay rights, 29
weeding out religious impurity, 105
See also Evangelical Christians
Christianity and the Social Crisis (Rauschenbusch), 138–139
Church and state separation
absence of, in US Constitution, 59
advantages, 170
advocacy organization monitoring, 171
importance to religious liberty, 166–172
influence on religions, 170
Jefferson, Thomas, advocacy, 22–23, 136

religious speech at school issue, 98
Santorum, Rick, opinion, 154
Williams, Roger, advocacy, 15, 16, 136
Church of England, 14
Civil disobedience, religious, 84–85
Civil law
binding of citizens institutions, 75
reason as common currency, 76
religious belief *vs.*, 74–75
Civil liberties organizations, 118
Civil Rights movement, 52
Civil War (US), 35
Clinton, Bill, 61
Coleman, John, 77–85
Colleges and universities, limitations on religion, 110
Congregationalists, 56
Constitutional federalism, 68–69
Cook, Marta, 135–140

D

The Daily Beast (website), 35
Daugherty v. Vanguard Charter School Academy (2000), 97
Day, Dorothy, 137
De La Motta, Jacob, 145
Declaration of Independence
Carroll, Charles, signatory, 110
Jefferson, Thomas, preamble, 56
rights granted by, 22, 36, 79
terminology elimination, 108
Declaration on Religious Freedom (Second Vatican Council), 80

Deism, 148–149

Democracy in America (Tocqueville), 57

Des Moines Independent Community School District, Tinker v. (1969), 98

DiNardo, Daniel N., 128–129

Doe, Santa Fe Independent School Dist. v. (2000), 89

Dolan, Timothy M., 130–131

E

Eastern Michigan University, 110

EEOC, Hosanna-Tabor v. (2012), 41–42, 60, 149

Egypt, religious liberty violence, 18

Enlightenment liberalism, 136

Establishment Clause (First Amendment)
  Catholic Church disagreement, 136
  description, 15, 18, 72–73, 92, 154–155
  free-exercise clause link, 81, 143
  priority of Founders, 18
  reading/interpretations, 60–61, 62
  religious group reminders, 79
  school prayer issue, 90
  Supreme Court ruling, 98–99
  violations, 84, 90
  West Cranston prayer banner violation, 72–73

Ethics and Public Policy Center/ Institute, 31, 161

European Union, 50–51

Evangelical Christians
  alliance with Roman Catholics, 159, 163
  avoidance of secular politics, 29
  campaign against LGBTQ equality, 29–30, 158, 163
  challenges to reproductive rights, 158
  First Great Awakening movement/persecution, 56–57
  ignoring of a federal law, 113–114
  itinerant preachers, 56–57
  origin in America, 56

Exemption laws, religious, 83–84

F

Faith-based organizations, 41

Family Research Council, 30–31, 159

Federalism, 68–69

Federalist Paper #10 (Madison), 145–146

First Amendment (US Constitution)
  amendments, 69–70
  codification/ratification, 56
  complexity of interpretation, 77–85
  description/meaning, 15, 31, 57, 59, 96, 115
  first words, 57
  Founders and, 110, 136, 142, 146
  historical understanding, 59
  Jefferson, Thomas, contributions, 23, 155
  misuse of, 31

NYPD surveillance violations, 125

Obama, Barack, purported rejection, 110

protective legislative acts, 107

religious discrimination debate, 31

religious freedom protections, 39

Santorum, Rick, statement, 153

student free speech protections, 95, 100–101

Supreme Court protections, 60–61, 62

treasuring of, by US Catholics, 79–80

See also Establishment clause; Free Exercise clause

First Great Awakening, 56

Forum on Religion and Public Life (Pew Research Center), 45

Founders of the United States

belief in religious faith for citizens, 39

beliefs in Deism, 148–149

First Amendment opinions, 110, 136, 142, 146

Obama, Barack, opinion, 66, 67

religious liberty model, 22, 23, 40–41, 63

sacrifices made by, 63

understanding of religion, 40

See also individual founders

Fourteenth Amendment (US Constitution), 69, 100

Franklin, Benjamin, 39

Free Exercise clause (First Amendment)

description, 18, 79

establishment clause link, 81, 143

Friedersdorf, Conor, 116–126

Fundamentalist Christians, 46, 113, 115

G

George, Henry, 138

George, Robert P., 161

Good News Club v. Milford Central School District (2001), 95

Great American Experiment, 57

Green, David, 173–176

Grote Industries, 113

Ground Zero mosque (New York, NY), 66–67

H

Halpin, John, 135–140

Hamilton, Alexander, 39

Haynes, Charles, 99

Health Care Conscience Rights Act, 107

Hercules Industries, 108

HIV, 168, 169

Hobby Lobby

opposition to Affordable Care Act birth control provision, 114–115

seeking of Affordable Care Act religious exemption, 160

Hosanna-Tabor v. EEOC (2012), 41–42, 60, 149

Houston, Tony, 71–76

Hutchinson, Sara, 166–172

I

I Have a Dream speech (King), 56
International Religious Freedom Act (US), 25
International Society for Human Rights, 46
Iran, restriction of religious freedom, 25
Islam, 67, 70, 134

J

Jay, John, 39
Jefferson, Thomas, 16
    advocacy for church/state separation, 22–23, 136
    belief in religious faith, 39
    belief in religious freedom for citizens, 39
    De La Motta, Jacob, letter, 145
    Deist beliefs, 148
    early biography, 16
    freedom of conscience advocacy, 59, 136
    letter to Danbury Baptists, 154
    stance against right to religious exercise, 68
    US Constitution preamble, 56
    wall of separation metaphor, 81–82
Jews/Judaism
    ban on religious practices, 46
    common Call to Conscience, 164–165
    discrimination allowance, 32
    forced intermarriage, 33
    Obama, Barack, and, 107–108
    Prohibition exemption, 83
    religious liberty activism, 31

religious persecution, 105
stance against idolatry, 78
support of Catholics, 80
John Paul II (Pope), 47, 50
John XXIII (Pope), 48

K

K&L Contractors, 113
King, Martin Luther, Jr., 56, 137
Kuligowski, Monte, 65–70

L

Laycock, Douglas, 30, 161
Lee v. Weisman (1992), 89
Leo XIII (Pope), 136, 139
LGBTQ (lesbian, gay, bisexual, transgender, queer)
    Catholic anti-LGBTQ campaign, 158
    Christian Right attacks, 159–162
    evangelical anti-LGBTQ campaign, 163
    limits on freedom, 162–163
    support by liberals and progressives, 163–165
    See also Same-sex marriage
Liberty Institute, 31
Limbaugh, David, 152–156
Lincoln, Abraham, 56
Lynn, Barry W., 111–115

M

Madison, James, 14, 16
    belief in religious freedom for citizens, 39
    freedom of conscience advocacy, 136

role in Bill of Rights, 142, 146
stance for more religious factions, 142
stance for religious liberty, 21–22
Mahony, Roger, 84
Marriage
Catholic viewpoint, 42, 159
Christian effort at redefining, 109
significance to Americans, 27
traditional, defined, 35, 36–37
See also Same-sex marriage
Marshall, Jennifer A., 20–27
Massachusetts Bay Colony, 14
McConnell, Michael W., 82
Memorial and Remonstrance Against Religious Assessments (Madison), 21–22, 142, 146
Mergens, Westside School District v. (1990), 98, 99
Michaelson, Jay, 28–33, 157–165
Milford Central School District, Good News Club v. (2001), 95
Miller, Samuel, 68
Minnesota, same-sex marriage issue, 33
Moschella, Melissa, 58–64
Mother Teresa, 47
Murray, John Courtney, 80
Muslims
anti-Muslim sentiment, 82
banning/regulation of church building, 68
majority presence in Turkey, 105
Obama, Barack, Egypt speech, 134
See also American Muslims
Myanmar, restriction of religious freedom, 25

N

National Prayer Day, 108
National Prayer Vigil for Life, 128, 131
New York Police Department (NYPD)
infringement on civil rights, 126
secret Demographics Unit, 118
Stop and Frisk policy, 117
surveillance of Muslims, 116–126
New York Times (newspaper), 82
Newland, Bill, 108
Newseum Institute, 99
No Child Left Behind law (2001), 99
Noonan, John, 51–52
North Korea
oppressive living conditions, 105
restriction of religious freedom, 25
USCIRF report, 104

O

Obama, Barack
Cairo University speech, 134
mosque-building rights of Muslims, 67
platitudes for religious freedom, 110
religious liberty and, 107–108
Ryan, Paul, stance against, 30
Obamacare. See Affordable Care Act
Orthodox Judaism, 31

P

Pattison, Mark, 127–131
Pew Research Center
    Forum on Religion and Public
        Life, 45–46
    Rising Restrictions on Religion
        report, 104
Picarello, Anthony, 159
Pierce v. Society of Sisters (1925),
    80
Pledge of Allegiance, 60, 73, 81
Politics, complementarity with
    religions, 174–175
Politics, liberal and progressive
    early Catholic Church opposi-
        tion, 136
    mark left by religious activ-
        ism, 137
    protection of liberty, democ-
        racy, 135–140
    support for LGBTQ, 163–165
Prayer
    Jefferson, Thomas, national
        day, 68
    Supreme Court ruling, 97–99
    West Cranston prayer banner
        violation, 72–73
    See also School expressions of
        religion
Presbyterians, 56
Progress and Poverty (George), 138
Puritans, 14–15

Q

Quakers, 56

R

Racial slavery, 35
Radio and TV preachers, 113

Ramadan, 66
Rauschenbusch, Walter, 137, 138–
    139
Religion Clause (First
    Amendment), 69
Religious civil disobedience, 84–85
Religious diversity
    encouragement of, 145–146
    promotion of secularism,
        143–144
Religious exemption laws, 83–84
Religious Freedom Day, 107
Religious Freedom Project
    (Newseum Institute), 99
Religious Freedom Restoration Act
    (RFRA), 59, 61, 63–64, 107
Religious liberty
    absence of constitutional
        guarantee, 65–70
    activism, 31, 137
    as a code word, 30–31
    conservative campaign meth-
        ods, 159–161
    as cornerstone of US life,
        21–22
    damage to religion, 141–151
    defense of, 34–37
    First Amendment commen-
        tary complexity, 77–85
    global restriction data, 26
    importance of church, state
        separation, 166–172
    increasing liberal support,
        170–172
    necessity for a free society,
        20–27
    Pew Research Center report,
        45
    Pledge of Allegiance lawsuit,
        60, 73, 81
    promotion of stability, 51

promotion of world peace,
equity, 44–53

public *vs.* private expressions,
25–27

US Constitution guarantee,
71–76

US Constitution protections,
27, 58–64

US model, 38–43, 41, 51–52,
59

Religious liberty bullies

anti-bullying initiatives, 74

fight against LGBTQ equality,
28–33

*The "Religious Liberty" Bullies and
Their Fight Against LGBT Equality* (Michaelson), 35

Reproductive health of women, 31

Rerum Novarum encyclical (Pope
Leo XIII), 139–140

Rhode Island Catholic establishment, 72

Rising Restrictions on Religion
(Pew Research Center), 104

Robertson, Pat, 113

Roosevelt, Eleanor, 52

Ryan, John, 137, 140

Ryan, Paul, 30

S

Same-sex marriage

Christian right opposition, 29,
37, 155, 158, 159, 161

denial of rights and benefits,
167

fight for racial equality comparison, 34–36

Michaelson, Jay, stance, 35

non-recognition by states, 31,
33, 161

recognition exemption efforts,
75, 83, 161, 163–164

societal accommodation of
rights, 84

See also LGBTQ (lesbian, gay,
bisexual, transgender, queer)

*Santa Fe Independent School Dist.
v. Doe* (2000), 89

Santorum, Rick, 153, 154

School, expressions of religion

allowed, 86–93

athletic team prayer, 91

classroom vocal prayer/Bible
reading, 87–88

equal access neutrality message, 99

moment of silence, 88

not allowed, 94–101

prayer at school events, 87–90,
93

protection of student expression, 100–101

rights of student-led prayer,
87

school personnel and prayer,
90–91

See You at the Pole
(organization), 95–101

student rights to pray, 87,
92–93

Supreme Court and, 97–99

teacher prayer participation,
93

teaching creationism, restriction, 92

unconstitutionality of religious expression, 94–101

Sears, Alan, 106–110

Second Vatican Council, 45, 46–
47, 52, 80

Secularism, 129, 143–145, 164

See You at the Pole (SYATP) student organization
  Daugherty v. Vanguard Charter Academy lawsuit, 97
  description, 95–96
  Establishment Clause nonapplicability, 99
  event advertising protections, 100–101
Segregation laws, 36
Separation of church and state. *See* Church and state separation
September 11, 2001, terrorist attacks, 66, 118, 167
Sharia laws, 67
Sherbert v. Werner (1963), 82
Smith, Al, 80
Societies
  common good/common values, 49, 50–51
  faith and communities, 40–41
  finding common values, 48–49
  governing/civil rights, 47
  human rights, 49–50
  necessity for religious liberty, 20–27
Society of Sisters, Pierce v. (1925), 80
Spinoza, Benedict, 147–149
Starr, Ellen Gates, 137
Stop and Frisk policy (NYPD), 117
Supreme Court
  amendment process powers, 70
  Constitutional amendments, 66, 69–70
  Daugherty v. Vanguard Charter School Academy, 97

First Amendment enforcement, 92
First Amendment protections, 60–61
Fourteenth Amendment activism, 69
Good News Club v. Milford Central School District, 95
health insurance law decision, 32
Hosanna-Tabor v. EEOC, 41–42, 60, 149
judicial activism (1925), 69
Lee v. Weisman, 89
ministerial exemption reaffirmation, 60
moment of silence decision, 88
Pierce v. Society of Sisters, 80
religious liberty case, 161
Santa Fe Independent School Dist. v. Doe, 89
school prayer decision, 90–91, 94–101
Sherbert v. Werner decision, 82
Tinker v. Des Moines Independent Community School District, 98
Westside School District v. Mergens, 98, 99
Wisconsin v. Yoder decision, 82

T

Thames, Knox, 104
Theological-Political Treatise (Spinoza), 147
Tinker v. Des Moines Independent Community School District (1969), 98
Title VII, Civil Rights Act, 82
Tocqueville, Alexis de, 53, 57

Tomasi, Silvano M., 44–53
Trinitarianism, 148

U

UN Human Rights Council, 51
Unitarianism, 148
United States (US)
 basis of diplomacy, 27
 Civil Rights movement, 52, 82
 experiment in religious liberty, 51–53
 founding principles, 14
 International Religious Freedom Act, 25
 National Prayer Day, 108
 No Child Left Behind law, 99
 pressure on foreign countries, 134
 promotion of freedom commitment, 25
 Religious Freedom Day, 107
 religious liberty court debates, 18
 religious liberty foundation, 38–43, 51–52, 59
 religious liberty model, 41
 religious roots, 22–23
 segregation era, 36
 September 11, 2001, terrorist attacks, 66, 118, 167
 Title VII, Civil Rights Act, 82
 See also Founders of the United States; Supreme Court
United States Conference of Catholic Bishops, 60
Universal Declaration of Human Rights, 24, 52

Universal Periodical Review of States (UN Human Rights Council), 51
US bishops' Committee on Pro-Life Activities, 128
US Commission on International Religious Freedom (USCIRF), 39, 104
US Conference of Catholic Bishops (USCCB)
 co-opting of legal professors, 30
 First Amendment rights, 60, 83
 focus of religious liberty campaign, 159
 separation of church/state beliefs, 166–172
US Constitution
 Fourteenth Amendment, 69
 Madison, James, ideas, 16
 minority protection from the majority, 74
 mosque-banning rights, 68–69
 ratification assurance, 67–68
 religious liberty guarantee, 71–76
 religious liberty limitations, 65–70
 religious liberty priorities, 18
 religious liberty protections, 27, 58–64
 school expressions of religion, restrictions, 86–93
 See also Bill of Rights; Church and state separation; First Amendment
US Court of Appeals, 81, 96, 113

US Department of Health and Human Services (HHS)
Affordable Care Act mandates, 42, 60, 143–144
contraception/sterilization mandate, 128
lawsuits, 37
Sebelius, Kathleen, announcement, 129
withdrawal of Catholic Relief Services contract, 83
US State Department, 25, 50–51
US Third Circuit Court of Appeals, 96

V

Vanguard Charter School Academy, Daugherty v. (2000), 97

W

Washington, George
belief in religious faith for citizens, 39
observation of religious freedom, 21
statement on scruples of men, 59
Weisman, Lee v. (1992), 89
Werner, Sherbert v. (1963), 82
West Cranston (RI) prayer banner, 71, 72–73
Westside School District v. Mergens (1990), 98, 99
Wiker, Benjamin, 141–151
Williams, Roger
advocacy for church/state separation, 15, 16, 136
arrival in Massachusetts Bay Colony, 14
drafting of document of governance, 15
Wisconsin v. Yoder (1980), 82
Woonsocket (RI) cross incident, 72, 73–74
World peace, 44–53

Y

Yoder, Wisconsin v. (1980), 82